# MOSHE KASHER

CHILDHO... ...DULTHOOD AT 16

# CONTENTS

## CHAPTER 1

"THE DAYZ OF WAYBACK"

## CHAPTER 2

"GET IN WHERE YOU FIT IN"

## CHAPTER 3

"THE CHRONIC"

## CHAPTER 4

"N.Y. STATE OF MIND"

## CHAPTER 5

"IN MY NEIGHBOURHOOD"

**CHAPTER 6**

*"THINGS DONE CHANGED"*

**CHAPTER 7**

*"SORTA LIKE A PSYCHO"*

**CHAPTER 8**

*"ILLEGAL BUSINESS"*

**CHAPTER 9**

*"IT'S ALL BAD"*

**CHAPTER 10**

*"WHO AM I?"*

**CHAPTER 11**

*"FREE"*

# CHAPTER 1

## "THE DAYZ OF WAYBACK"

I was born unattractive. Babies are unattractive. At least, that's what I've always assumed. Pruny little creatures. The final seconds of prenatal pleasure come to a screeching halt as a nasty little thing is bungeed into the world. It pierces her heart. When Mommy hears that howl, she forgets about her first thought. "My son!" is all she can think about right now. My mother had never heard that scream. My mother is hard of hearing.

According to my mother, I was born out of control, a feral child with a wild heart who was physiologically incapable of dealing with the force and ferocity of my own body. If you could see my small Jew body right now, you'd find it difficult to believe. When the slightest thing didn't go my way, I'd snarl and snap, bite and foam, shake with hatred, and my body would spasm in convulsions of rage and uncontrollable passion. My mother, terrified, referred me to a therapist. I was four years old at the time. That is a turning point in my life. I was led into the therapeutic garden and left to roam, passing through an ancient rusted gate guarded by Freud and Jung's ghosts. Being told that you require therapy while still moist from the womb practically breaks a boy.

**April 18th: Bea and the boys leave to California**

Every day we were gone was marked with an X. Each day passed as he waited to see his family again. I think he eventually concluded, sick to his stomach, "They aren't coming back."

The X's eventually stopped. My life in Oakland began when the X's ceased. We immediately moved in with my granny. Hope, my mother's mother. There was never any thought of returning. We were three alone in Oakland, sleeping in my grandmother's living room. My mother was unable to find a job. The system is completely skewed against deaf people. Would you consider hiring one?

Every problem my mother had, she blamed on my father. Vocally. Loudly. He was to blame for all of her problems. My mother would cook us a bad meal or refuse us chocolates, and she would point east and sign, "Your father!" My brother, who had a very vivid recall of his relationship with my father, was unaffected by this kind of poisoning of the parental well. My mother, on the other hand, was able to transform my father's image into a kind of malevolent phantom, hovering behind us at all times, taking fun things from our fingertips.

My mother would count my father's holiday gifts for my brother and me, and if David received even one more chocolate than I did, she would hold them out and exclaim, "See? Your father adores your little brother more than he does you!" Those remarks would break my heart. I assumed my mother was telling the truth because I couldn't grasp the tiny pettiness of ex-lovers (having rarely taken any at the time). I didn't see why he preferred David. So, David has always had a stronger chin than me.

David truly outperformed me in every way. According to the biblical character arc, he was the firstborn son in a Jewish family, and he played the hero perfectly. My older brother was born with the skills to traverse the churning white water of my parents' river of rage. I simply drowned. He was born an ideal quiet statesman. The ideal son. The ideal pupil. The ideal Jew. He represented everything I wasn't. While others examined me with microscopes to determine what was wrong with me, they only ever pointed to what he was doing correctly. That was not his fault. He was playing the part that made him feel secure in the insane world into which we were both born. In truth, David and I would cuddle together on quiet nights and wonder how this was our existence.

Meanwhile, my mother's hatred toward my father rose as our circumstances deteriorated.

The poorer we were, the more blatantly she slandered him, and the more she despised him. When my father's mother, Helen Kasher, grew ill with Parkinson's disease, he begged her to let me come to New York to see her before she became too sick to communicate. My mother responded by informing my father that no visitation had been agreed upon and, as a result, I would not be visiting. As a result, I have no recollection of my baba. There is no memory. Nothing but wisps and phantoms.

My father's fictional enemy eventually held us back financially so badly that we had to go on welfare. That's how the food stamps got there. Food stamps and government aid are both available. Welfare recipients are Jews. That is unusual. Such as witnessing a leprechaun. We would have granted you wishes if you could have caught us in the wild. This was, by the way, old welfare. Before it was filtered to avoid embarrassment. The food stamp is now but a relic of a bygone era. To maintain dignity, poor families are now given a discrete-looking card that cannot be distinguished from a credit card. What nonsense. These days, underprivileged and impoverished youth have things so easy. In my day, the food stamp was a real stamp, both humiliating and daring. Lightly coloured so as not to be confused with actual money (which we poor people didn't have). It was larger than an ordinary dollar, similar to a Confederate bill. The face of MC Hammer was on the twenty-dollar stamp, gazing back at you with enormous white fangs. Every time my mother took them out, there was a trail of tears, the white note screaming, "Poor family here! Sneak a peek while you can! They can't even afford to eat!"

Kermit the Frog could have popped out of my mother's wallet in a top hat, dancing a soft shoe, and singing "Welfare!" What a disgrace. When the public assistance department discovered we were Jewish, we were appointed a counsellor to help us cope with the trauma. In order to avoid being harassed, we were given a plaque and a special access at the back of the welfare office. Of course, I wasn't just Jewish; I was extremely Jewish. I spoke Yiddish. To my mother's chagrin, my father and the judicial system notified her when I was seven that she would have to let my brother and I return to New York for visitation. I grudgingly returned to my hometown to see the man who abused me, the man who didn't love me like he adored my brother. Of course, I was enraged. Of course, I worshipped him a little. I returned to New York to discover that, during my absence, he had joined the Satmars, a Chassidic group. My father had always admired the Chassis. The Ultra-Orthodox kids and the truly pious kids played dodgeball in Sea Gate. In essence, English speakers vs. dead-language lovers. Because their legs were slightly atrophic from years of yeshiva study by day and high-chicken-fat diets by night, the pasty old-worlders should have been rather easy to bean. This is the part of the story where I'm meant to become a local hero because my secular athletic abilities helped us win the neighbourhood championship. But I was overweight and out of shape. I was winded, then got blasted by the ball as screams of "Hit the goy!" echoed in my head. I found a well of terror to jump into around that time. I ached because I felt so different. I'd been in therapy for years at that point, despite the fact that I was only seven years old; I just knew something was profoundly wrong with me. I grew concerned with the possibility that someone would figure out what was going on and expose me to the broken piece of human machinery that I was. Everything frightened me. My ferocious howling gradually gave way to a pool of terror. I seamlessly shifted from angry out-of-control youngster to terrified out-of-control kid. I was seven years old and convinced I was a jerk. My father was of little assistance. He sent me to a Chabad (another, slightly more user-friendly sect of Chassidism) day camp to "learn the ropes' ' of Hasidic Judaism after he saw how lost I was in Sea Gate. This is akin to sending your illiterate, developmentally handicapped child to Yale instead of Harvard and smirking at the concession you've made. He simply didn't get it.

"Don't worry about the kids making fun of you, just act like you know what you are doing."

"But, Dad, I have no idea what I'm doing." "I can't pray in Hebrew if I don't know Hebrew," I'd reply, hoping against hope that logic would save me from another day of mouthing along to Hebrew prayers, my prayer book upside down, praying no one saw I wasn't saying anything at all.

"I don't know how to hear either, but I fool people all the time." You just pretend to be Jewish like I pretend to be hearing."

My father had a pet fascination with how "undeaf" he appeared to be. Until the day he died, he was sure that no matter how many times his questions and queries were met with "Huh?" he was deceiving them; that despite his twisted Charlie Brown's teacher voice, no one noticed he couldn't hear.

# CHAPTER 2

## "GET IN WHERE YOU FIT IN"

In first grade, I met Richard Lilly. He was one of the only white students in my class, and we quickly became best friends. I'm not sure how youngsters make friends when they're lacking in personality. What did we discover in common?

"Hey, I have an incredibly small white penis; do you?"

We somehow connected and became inseparable from then on. Perhaps our connection was unconscious. His family was just as dysfunctional as mine, but we never talked about it that way. Richard also lived with his grandmother. His father was an alcoholic, and his mother was a crack addict prostitute. We were two troubled white teenagers struggling to keep our heads above water. My mother would read to us from a blue-covered booklet called Boys and Sex.

Every Tuesday, we would spend hours praying for comets to strike the house and put us out of our agony while my mother droned on about "orgasms" and "rectal insertion." As she spoke, our disgust gave way to a buzzing weariness. She somehow took all of the pleasure out of it. Never before has a nine-year-old been so bored by sex.

Every talk ended with the same question: "Are either of you gay?" My mother was overly supportive of homosexuality, if such a thing exists. We had the clear sensation that being gay was not only acceptable, but also preferred.

"Are either of you gay?"

"No, Mom," we'd say again, "we still aren't fucking gay."

I'd been looking forward to middle school for a long time. A strange thing when you consider that middle school is one of the most horrible environments on earth. In terms of torturous social environments the order goes:

Holocaust (various)

Siberian Gulag

Middle School

Iron Maiden (torture device or concert)

After coming perilously near failing fifth grade, I entered Claremont Middle School full of excitement and hope. I was on my way to an awkward prepubescent adolescence. The world appeared to be my undeveloped oyster. But now, with Richard gallivanting with wealthy cheerleaders (as I imagined), I was abruptly alone, friendless, and on the verge of social exile. Claremont was clearly divided along racial and class lines, as I rapidly discovered. The semi-equality of elementary school vanished the moment it hit the Claremont blacktop. The responsibilities were clearly defined in this situation. I just wasn't sure where I belonged.

There were three categories of white folks at Claremont Middle School. There were the white individuals who made it to the popular group (a multiethnic power clique united by their contempt for others), the geeks, and the fuckups.

A word about geeks. These aren't the stereotypical nerds you may imagine. They aren't bespectacled losers with acne so thick that their Dungeons and Dragons bespoke pocket protectors aren't visible. I'm not defending them; rather, I'm clarifying. Nerd mostly just meant white. For some reason, the colour white stirred up thoughts of squares and losers in Claremont's mind. So the nerds, who would have been "people" at any other school, became the bottom rung of the social ladder at Claremont.

There was variation among black people. There was the churchgoer, the clown, the thug, the ladies' man, the crack dealer, the oft-failed, the gay dude, the African, big-ass muthafucka, retard, rapist, nice to whites, hella tall, half Asian, knows karate, has a twin, black with freckles, going to college, and more, and more. However, if you were white, you were simply white.

Unless you're a jerk. Fuckups were not white; they were just fuckups. It was as if you didn't see their whiteness because the dysfunction was so loud that you couldn't focus on anything else. They were the kids their mothers warned them to avoid. The students who can be found at the back of any school campus. These were the white guy terrors of Claremont Middle School.

# CHAPTER 3

# "THE CHRONIC"

Donny began showing me around the men in Oakland. A sloppy little gang of true-blue jerks. They formed the P.A.G., a small proto-street gang that stood for "Pure Adrenaline Gangsters." It was such a ridiculous name that it should have been called the Pure Hard-core Adrenaline Gangsters. P.H.A.G. It was a shattered group of youngsters. They all come from divorced houses, and I mean every single one of them. The majority are from messed-up, abusive relationships. Donny showed me around. There were DJ and Corey, two brothers with such disproportionate proportions that they reminded me of Arnold Schwarzenegger and Danny DeVito from the movie Twins. DJ was big and incapable of having a violent notion without quickly acting on it with his fists. He carried penny rolls wrapped in duct tape with him to augment the force and weight that his fists bore. He was the Don Corleone to Donny's Luca Brasi. Corey, on the other hand, was like the group's Joe Pesci. Little, obnoxious, and always starting trouble. He was a few years older than us but a few years less mature, so everything worked out well.

Terry Candle, or Monk as he was more well known, was a half-Japanese boy with a fastidious intellect and a mother with significant links to Northern California marijuana farmers. He was given the moniker Monk because he was never seen without a thick hooded sweatshirt pulled up over his head, giving him the appearance of a very small Benedictine drug dealer. His mother's connection to those pot-growing hippies up north made him the main dope salesman to the white-under-thirteen set in North Oakland, something I didn't realise at the time. There was also Jamie. Jamie James was a child so absurd that he appeared to have been manufactured by a screenwriter; with brilliant orange hair and a hideous teenage peach fuzz moustache, Jamie resembled a clown. He also acted like one. He was a chronic liar. It was impossible to tell whether or not he was telling the truth about anything. As a result of his father's regular, brutal, man-sized beatings, his personality ultimately broke into so many pieces that he just picked them up and fashioned them into whatever matched the occasion best. Unfortunately, he did it poorly, and the result was a guy who could only be loved by the P.A.G. Having a habitual liar as a friend leaves you scarred. To this day, if I meet someone who tells too many weird stories, I presume they're lying and visualise a gentle orange halo surrounding their face like a patron saint of dishonesty. Guess who else was occasionally present? Joey! Imagine! The slayer of the Italian giant. He survived a fight with a black child. It was like a Jewish youngster in the 1960s getting to hang out with Sandy Koufax. I was in the company of my hero. I made an effort not to swoon. The boys gradually grew accustomed to my presence. As I walked through the Claremont halls, DJ would nod and ask, "'Sup?" I felt as if I'd been let in on a little secret. I'd been promoted after a few weeks of rare invites to sneak off across the block during lunch and smoke cigarettes with the boys. Donny approached me and asked me to meet him at his place after school that day. I'm not sure I'd have had the bravery to show up if I'd realised what I was getting myself into that day, but I'm also not sure I'd have had the courage not to. As I neared Donny's house, I unlatched the gate to his backyard.

"Donny?" I dialled.

As I turned the bend into the backyard, I saw DJ, Corey, Joey, and the rest of the gang standing there. Donny grabbed my arm and informed everyone that I had decided to join the P.A.G. I'd never done anything like that. I turned to face Donny. "Uh, Donny, uh… we haven't really discussed this in depth." I was a little worried, not sure if I was ready to become a full-fledged baby gangster. Donny simply winked at me. I drank a long gulp as I gazed about at this motley crew of white bad boys. These were the kids their mothers warned them about, and I was being asked to jump in with them. "It ain't nothin', homeboy," Jamie soothed me, speaking in the lilt of a character from a 1970s blaxploitation film.

DJ sighed and whispered, "He's too fucking scared."

Jamie wrapped his arm around my waist and whispered, more like an old-school travelling hippie this time, "Just be cool and go with it."

Joey, who wasn't really a part of the group but was more of an outside consultant, just smoked and observed me. I'd seen it before. I was being evaluated. The tribal warriors were testing me to determine if I was brave enough to be one of them, much like Kevin Costner in Dances with Wolves. I knew exactly what I had to do. I took a step forward, crouched into the horse position of Tae Kwon Do, took a deep breath, and declared, "I am ready to join."

Everyone burst out laughing. However, no one asked me to leave. It was not easy to join. I had to join like five fucking times over the next few weeks. The problem with the gang was that it wasn't actually a gang at all, but rather a term for the group of jerks into which I had fallen. In truth, the name represented the final vestige of our youth. It had a childish moniker, reminiscent of the "He Man Woman Haters Club" from The Little Rascals. The affiliation was more important than the name. The issue with it not being a "real" gang was that the regulations were somewhat vague. Particularly the rules governing how to join.

Every P.A.G. The initiation ritual I went through was deemed insufficient thereafter, and I'd be asked to undertake another pain ritual or sexual humiliation in order to be approved. I poked my finger up my ass and tried to write my name in crap on the wall; I smacked my little adolescent dick on an ice-cold school bench; I drank a dead goldfish; and I smoked on my arm. It was the width of a Camel. I fucking remember that, and believe me, you would as well. As this fresh group of guys surrounded me, I pressed the lit end of this cigarette into my forearm and shuddered in anguish as my flesh boiled and smoked. All the guys applauded and clapped me on the back for what felt like the best decision I'd ever made at the time. The burn immediately became infected, but I was afraid to ask for help in case the FBI was called in to investigate the P.A.G., so I just slapped a Band-Aid on it and prayed for the best. It was putrescent and coated gold a month later, and my arm felt like a fifty-pound water balloon. It only ached when I moved it, smiled, chatted, pointed it downward or upward, or breathed, so I assumed it was fine.

I flew home a few weeks later to see my father in Brooklyn. He finally mentioned something about the Band-Aid that never came off after staring at it for a time. He forced me to show him, and then vomited on my arm. Perhaps that did not occur. He did, however, force me to go to the hospital so that my arm may be saved from gangrene or amputation. What a jerk my father was.

Worse, the P.A.G. folded two months after my trial by fire. Nothing changed, we were still hanging around and doing the same things we did before the end of the P.A.G. era; they just decided that the gang was lame and that it was over. I suppose I should have been grateful. My next induction ceremony was rumored to include ritual rape. Despite everything, I never regretted getting burned. Over the years, I'd gaze down at the scar and smile a little, remembering the moment I burned my way to fuckup.

After a period of hanging out with these men, I discovered they were using marijuana. Pot. Our parents referred to it as grass, but we referred to it as damp. They named it The Chronic if it was particularly good. The D.A.R.E. The program referred to it as a gateway drug. I decided that if they asked, I'd smoke with those men. Stupid marijuana! The nation laughed at Bill Clinton when he said he didn't inhale. No, I didn't. When I first used marijuana, I felt more connected to Bill Clinton than to the black community. I tried my hardest. At that point, I'd been smoking cigarettes for months, but the only time I'd inhaled was when I mistakenly swallowed a mouthful of smoke. I imagined that was how people got lung cancer: one too many unintentional inhalations. It couldn't be what you were supposed to be doing, could it? I just wanted to look cool in front of those men, but I had no idea what I was doing. With no knowledge of anatomy or science, I propose that allowing smoke into your lungs is an unnatural act. That is why many die as a result of smoke inhalation. So when Donny invited me to smoke some pot in the bushes and I didn't get high, it was my lungs, not me. I was serious. My lungs became infected.

I didn't want to mess things up in case I wasn't invited to the fuckup birthday celebration. Little did I realise that the fuckups don't throw parties; they ruin other people's. They also don't like to lose pals. Friends do not leave because they are asked to. It takes a lot of courage to be one of these guys. You must be willing to be robbed, beaten, and have your parents' house sacked, among other things. In exchange, you get a gang of motherfuckers that will rob or beat the s*** out of anyone on your behalf at any time. That meant a great deal to me. That meant everything. So when my pansy-ass lungs refused to cooperate, I freaked out a little. I needed these folks to understand that I was serious. So, like no other woman I've ever been with, I pretended. To be honest, I wasn't certain I wasn't high. Maybe this was it, maybe marijuana felt just like not smoking marijuana, and you just felt cool and tough for doing it. I walked from that bush to my grandmother's car, which was waiting to pick me up after school, and I attempted to convince myself that I had changed, that I had gotten high. But it wasn't until I fired up the next time that I realised how incorrect I'd been.

Tommy Klark's residence was where I first went high for real. His older brother passed me a joint, and my lungs opened up to the smoke portal that allowed me to enter a new realm. I floated away as the THC drizzled its thick syrupy covering over my brain. So this is how it feels to be high… I smoked and smoked, as each hit chipped away at another aspect of my existence... puff puff... my troubles were gone. What was there to be concerned about when it was Ganja Time? Puff puff, my retardation was gone; I could puff away the extra chromosome and felt my Down syndrome turn into a Down Situation... puff puff, dammit I was clever! Even if I wasn't, I was smart! Puff puff, my fat is gone! I had nice, sculpted muscles someplace under there. Puff puff, my dread of being rejected by the cool kids was gone. I'd gotten way beyond the cool kids by jumping into a Mario warp zone. Fuck those squat squares of garbage. I didn't need or want to be popular, and I didn't want to be anything. All I wanted was to get high with these men for the rest of my life. I'm not sure if there is a heaven, but if there is, it has to resemble something like Tommy's backyard.

After that, things become murky. We began to drink Everclear margaritas. For the uninitiated, Everclear is essentially potable rubbing alcohol. It's 99 percent alcohol, and as you sip it, you can feel your afflicted trachea crumble. I ate a Popsicle with salt on top. It was the most delectable dish I'd ever had. Someone played "While the City Sleeps," by Mc 900 Foot. We all slam danced around the room until we collapsed in a heap, including Jesus. I've never had a better night in my life. I had no notion that was what had been wrong all along until I got high. It wasn't because my parents were deaf. It wasn't because I had a frantic furious mother or a zealous absent father. It wasn't because I was obese and retarded, or because I was insane, furious, Jewish, or anything else. I simply needed to get high. Nobody ever tells you that when you're a youngster. That it feels fucking fantastic. They tell you that you're loopy and disoriented, but no one tells you that it crawls through your flesh, filling in every gaping hole where your humanity failed to fuse. Euphoria's thick molten lava fills the cracks of your psyche, and you understand your soul was an electric blanket that hadn't been plugged in until now. Parents and therapists never warn you that you'll forget all the reasons you despise yourself. They don't tell you that nonsense because it will make everyone want to go high. That sensation—the numbing euphoria of self-medication—is what drives people to become drug addicts. Many people get high; just a few become addicts. It is not the act of getting high that makes you an addict, but what the act of getting high does to you. If you start low and work your way up, you will eventually reach normal. Loaded feels good, but if it's the first time you've ever felt good in your life, you're in big trouble. That's what I was after. It wasn't the high; it was the knowledge that everything was well. Is that correct?

Getting high for the first time was similar to seeing for the first time. It was as if I'd been wearing blinders my entire life, and with that first hit, they flew off and I saw the world for the first time in its entirety. Before that initial hit, the world had seemed so narrow and myopic, and as I exhaled, I breathed the new vista before me. The universe grew indefinitely. I wasn't afraid of anything because it was bright and clear. I had the impression that I could see indefinitely. My life had been a gloomy, small, little place until that time, with all of the individuals who dominated me dictating the rules and dynamics. I had no authority over anything. And then, all of a sudden, my universe opened up. I could see for miles and miles.

A few days later, I went to see Richard. I hopped on the BART train and gazed through the glass as the environment changed from Oakland's filth to Lafayette's gloss like an old-fashioned nickel arcade. I felt like a completely different person.

When I got there, I proposed to Richard that we go smoke cigarettes. He'd tried them and despised them, but agreed to do it anyhow. We sat on a hill, and I lit up a cigarette, took a hit, and passed it to him.

"You're inhaling it now, like my dad does," Richard observed, his voice a mix of admiration and fear.

"Ha, yeah, I learned how." I looked at my old pal, took a big breath, and admitted, "I smoked weed, too."

He looked at me, perplexed. "Wait, what?"

"I smoked weed, dude, and it was awesome." It's not what they say, you know? It felt fantastic. Like jerking off but cumming the entire time. It's insane."

Richard took it all in quietly, extinguished his cigarette, stood up, and said, "Promise me you won't do that ever again."

I burst out laughing. "C'mon, man, what are you talking about?"

"Fucking promise me!" he shouted, almost in tears.

I got a sense of how serious things were. For a split second, I glanced at my friend, unsure what to say. What could I possibly say?

"I'm afraid I can't do that, man. These are my only buddies in the world. It's different for you because you've got this amazing thing going on out here, where you're playing baseball and crap and making tons of friends, and I don't. Besides, everything they've been telling us about drugs is a lie. What's with the D.A.R.E. shit? It's nonsense. They simply do not want us to know the truth."

"What fucking secret?"

"Why don't you let me bring some by sometime and I'll show you."

Richard's expression turned angry, he remained silent for a long time, and then he murmured, "I can't be your friend if you do drugs." You must make a decision. It's either that or I."

Richard was never seen again.

# CHAPTER 4

# "N.Y. STATE OF MIND"

My brother and I flew back to New York shortly after my head had been blown wide by my unexpected experiences. Return to Sea Gate. Return to the past. Weed and drink had propelled my intellect into the future while my body flew back to the Stone Age. There was nowhere I would have preferred to be at that time. After being exposed to the joys of being high and then having them taken away from me with a summer trip back to the old country, it's no surprise that I was unhappy in New York. I needed something, so I had to settle for gulping deeply when Shabbos wine was served to me and engaging in late-night phone sex.

I'd discovered the pleasures of phone sex just before leaving California in the summer of 1991. My mother had long since had a 900 number block set on the phone line as a form of mental protection. Fortunately, the phone companies had devised a clever workaround for those 900 blockages, which I can't imagine wasn't a direct response to the dropping revenues generated by allowing parents to cut their children off phone sex. If you can't dial 900 numbers, how about calling a developing country? Small, distant countries had long-distance agreements that charged around $5 per minute for the connection. After paying a ten-dollar connection fee, these poor countries may begin scraping money off the penises of American hornballs.

I dialled Antigua and the Philippines and jerked my eager little dick in response to their groans and foul language. I puked in both Trinidad and Tobago. I brought cum rivers to drought-stricken islands. I e-JAH-culated upon Rastafarian marijuana plantations. I can picture those ladies now, six kids in a little tin shanty, cooking a goat curry stew with a baby on their hip while boredly moaning to me about how much they wanted my enormous cock. I didn't have a big cock yet, but I wasn't about to tell them that. I called every evening. My father would ask me to fetch him a cup of water and then touch his feet—a nonsexual but exceedingly strange request. More than anything, I felt like a royal subject. I'd wait until I heard snores to be sure everyone was asleep before sneaking downstairs to contact my tropical foreign queen. I once dialled a number and received an older Filipino voice on the other end of the line. It sounded strange. The voice of a granny.

" 'Allo?" The huskiness of the voice confused me, but my dick was tough and unfazed.

"I'm rock hard and ready for you," I said quietly, attempting to appear of legal age to make such a call. Nothing like a thirteen-year-old's squeaky adolescent creak to ruin a wonderful tropical jerk session.

"Oh. Sorry. Sorry. No. I don't make those kinds of calls."

"You don't what?" I didn't spend the $9.95 connection charge to be refused by a woman who said sorry. I double-checked the number to make sure I hadn't phoned it incorrectly. I hadn't done so. I chose to press the issue for whatever reason.

"C'mon, give it to me…" My voice cracked as I panted, showing my youthful excitement.

The hesitant phone whore spoke up. "Oh, okay, you want to puck me?"

I did. I truly did. I'd never wanted to puck someone more. That gruff old voice on the other end of the phone had softened a little.

"Yes, that's what I want; I want you to give it to me."

And then there was another tug of war with an island lady. I'm still not sure if I persuaded a random Filipino granny I'd misdialed to start a career in phone sex that day, or if I drew someone out of retirement for one last groan. All I know is that when the phone bill arrived, even that euphoric call was no longer worth it. My father summoned me into the kitchen, holding a phone bill up as if it were a subpoena. I was caught. I sank into my chair, waiting for the hellfire lecture to begin. I realised I hadn't given this much thought.

"The phone bill is fifteen hundred dollars this month," my father snarled at me, his nostrils flaring, his fury barely simmering beneath the surface. My father had this way of getting so enraged that you wished he'd just beat you and be done with it. I took notes on his form because he was a skilled rager. This could be useful someday.

I slouched in my seat even further. "Yeah, sorry about that."

My dad leaned into me and signed, "Phone sex?"

I shrugged. What could I do or say? My dad and the weight of the entire Jewish people were bearing down on me. I was fucked. At my circumcision ceremony when I was eight days old, Zeidi, then one hundred years old, embraced me in his withered hands and stated to my father and the Lord, "This boy will be a great rabbi, I can see into his soul."

Thirteen years later, I was telling my father about how I'd built up $1500 in expenses while pumping my dick in his living room. Perhaps Zeidi had been peering into the soul of someone else. Perhaps his soul-looking eyes were affected by glaucoma. I'm not certain. Conveniently, I had gotten roughly $1500 in Bar Mitzvah money from complete strangers invited by my father from the local

Jewish community. I'd never had so much money as that day after my Bar Mitzvah. But it was emptied on my penis the day after my Bar Mitzvah. I used up all of my Bar Mitzvah funds on phone sex. "Phone sex?" I envisioned God staring down at me, shaking his figurative head. You used your Bar Mitzvah funds for phone sex? The holy rite I instructed you to perform, you stole and wasted your money on calling 'Hot Island Bitches'?"

I'm ashamed to stare at God in his third, fiery eye. "I guess so. Yes, I mean it." God is scowling. "This does not please me." "I'm the one who lost all that money," I would insist. "Anyhow, isn't this a rite of passage into manhood?" What better way to mature than that?" God would mumble, "Well... I normally don't give in to arguments since I am an omnipotent perfectionist, but it is an excellent point." At the very least, I tried to persuade my father that this was how the talk would go. My father was not amused. The rest of my trip to New York was spent awkwardly mingling with my family, wishing for drugs or foreign voices, and watching my stepmother put away the phone at night. I tiptoed throughout the house, but I could tell what everyone was thinking: "Who is this pervert?" I was eager to return to Oakland.

# CHAPTER 5

# "IN MY NEIGHBOURHOOD"

With a sigh of relief, I returned to Oakland and went straight back to my old haunts. We spent our days and nights travelling about Oakland, seeking ridiculously exciting stuff to do. It's not easy being a thirteen-year-old outlaw. When you're so young, having blacklist fun is a constant challenge. A large portion of the work must be done at night. Some illegal activities were simple because no one would guess a guy with such a cherubic baby face of being such a badass. That's how we got away with bombings. Going bombing meant packing a backpack full of Krylon brand spray paint and heading out to cover the neighbourhood in graffiti. The harder you crushed a region, the more firmly you owned it. We controlled Rockridge and a large portion of North Oakland. Our tags covered every block, every empty spot, and every bus bench. Choosing a tag was a crucial and final step. It was similar to going on a Native American vision quest and returning with a spirit animal. Except that there are no redeeming spiritual lessons. Or perhaps an emotional voyage. Actually, it wasn't much like a vision quest at all. However, once you chose a tag, it became your identity, and your nom de plume was displayed on every bus in the East Bay.

We were always seated in the back of the bus. We did it in honour of Rosa Parks. No, we did it to avoid being tagged. Someone would give out a Magnum marker with a fat tip or a streaker, a grease paint pen that was nearly difficult to remove off a window once it dried. If we didn't have one of those tools, we used shoe polish bottles with big round sponges saturated in black polish that would flow down from the letters we wrote on the bus windows, lamenting our lack of creative skill. Alternatively, we would scratch our tags onto the windows with scribes, which were sandpaper-tipped drill bits. Anything we could do to get our names on the list. Did I mention I was a bad graffiti artist? I was. It was a cause of tremendous guilt for me, but I ignored it on a daily basis and tagged my way out of

Oakland regardless. Graffiti is classified into two types: quality and quantity. Being a fantastic artist might earn you recognition and praise, but if all you did was draw pretty pictures in your sketchbook, you would as well not have lived. Every day, I tried to figure out how to draw old-school, New York subway-style murals, but all I ever managed to depict were edgy piles of puke. So I chose number two. The village should be bombed. Literally. I scribbled my name all over the place. Every time I went out in the town, I scrawled my tag on whatever surface I could find. I felt great joy when I walked around my area and saw my defacing tags gazing back at me. The P.A.G. had evolved into a graffiti team known as UCF, or Unconvicted Felons. It's beyond me why people were so enamoured with illicit acronyms back then. Most graffiti crews had one. There were 640, a crew named after the penal code for vandalism; AS, or Altered States; the LORDS crew; and our opponents, BSK. It wasn't much of a rivalry, to be honest. BSK was a crew from our neighbourhood who was far more powerful than we could have imagined. They were a really frightening group of adolescents, with significant connections to Mexican gangs in East Oakland. If only we'd understood it before we started spewing nonsense. Someone at UCF had somehow crossed out one of their stickers that had appeared in our area. It was a symbol of our local domination to us. To BSK, it was a declaration of war. We were completely prepared for war until they arrived, an entire bus full of scary-looking students from classes above us.

The throng gathered in front of Claremont, armed with bats and bottles, ready to rumble. We took one glance at the army in front of the school and snuck out the rear door, disbanding the UCF. We reformed as SS, or Simply Savage, a new, war-free crew. I then advised that we not use an abbreviation that was similar to the Nazi secret police, so we changed it to IA, or Illegal Art. We weren't the most dedicated to our crew's moniker, but we were devoted to the concept of graffiti. We even endangered our lives one day by climbing into a train tunnel. Tunnels are beautiful. The act of man drilling a tunnel through a mountain is an extraordinary feat of human ingenuity. It's almost sexual in its penetration. (In fact, everytime I see a lady these days, I think to myself, "Man, I'd love to fortify her walls and use a boring machine to grind out a passageway that would allow transit to and from her ovaries."

There is and was something scary and intriguing about the dark mystery of the subway tunnel, and it didn't help that we had one gazing at us from the mountain that divided Oakland from the Contra Costa County suburbs. We often peered at the opening of that tunnel from the other side of the fence, wondering what secrets lie within.

We discovered it one day. DJ heard of a small room about a mile down the main tunnel that the BART train ripped through.

"A fucking room!" "A little fucking room!" DJ drooled again, his tongue moving faster than his brain.

I wasn't clear why we should be impressed. "I mean, aren't we in a room right now?" "What's the big deal?"

"The big deal is your fat belly, you little bitch." When DJ found a method to label me obese, he got slightly more expressive.

Of course, this was a little unfair. Fat teenagers do not have "fat bellies." Years of harrumphing, beer-swilling, and Salisbury steak-eating "gotta get away from my wife" nights are required to develop a huge fat male gut. I had a lovely boyish gel body. Pink puffy tits and hairless "never had love" handles. The Lakota Sioux referred to me as "Swims in a T-shirt." I wasn't overweight; I was undefined. DJ has a difficulty with nuance.

"You are a fat bitch!"

"Don't I know it!" I fired back, sliding into a comfortable game. "I actually met your mom at the fat bitch support group I go to."

DJ, out of choices, punched me in the chest.

"It'll be dope!" DJ went on, oblivious to my sobbing in the corner. "We can shoot over the fence and walk down into that room in single file to see what's inside." Plus, it's all new walls in there, and we could tag the whole fucking house. "Who's in?"

I didn't want to express what I was thinking, which was that I was terrified, so I just grumbled in a way that seemed tough and noncommittal to me. Donny, the mastermind behind our brainless scheme, appeared to be deep in concentration. I stared at him, attempting to psychically compel him to abandon the idea, and he appeared to be on the verge of doing so when he cocked his head to the side and said, "I've got weed." We'd be able to smoke there."

Preparations began right away. We trudged silently up to the entrance of the BART tunnel, as if going before a battlefield full with Vietcong. Villagers ran up to us in a single file as we passed past.

"You no go der!" they said as they blessed us with incense. "Bad tunnel, lots of enemies!" Never again, American!"

But we persisted.We arrived at the barbed-wire cyclone fencing and took in the signage put up to warn youth like us of such things. STOP! There were signs all over the place. DANGER IN THE TUNNEL!

NO, THIS IS NOT A GOOD IDEA.

FUCK IT THEN, I'M SURE YOU'RE GOING TO DIE.

Ignoring the warnings, we hopped over razor wire and through secondary security walls until we were at the mouth of the tunnel, a vast expanse of blackness sucking itself into the mountain. This was a terrible idea.

DJ, possibly too stupid to be scared, broke the silence by turning to face me and stating, "Fats, you at the end of the line." You're going to slow us down."

Fats agreed. We began our journey down the tunnel on a narrow emergency platform, feeling the wall for support and putting one foot in front of the other. From the rear of the line, I tried to keep up with everyone else, but the emptiness of the tunnel was hammering into my mind from behind. If it hadn't been for the electrified third rail threatening execution, I would have pissed myself. We'd gotten about a quarter-mile in, deep enough that we couldn't see the light from where we'd entered, when something strange happened. The air behind us warmed up and then sucked away, as if a suction hose had been attached to the other end of the tunnel. We came to a complete halt. The ground underneath us began to rumble, and two dazzling eyes blinked, greeting from the darkness. The train conductor blew his horn, and we heard a loud, shrieking, distorted beep.

Someone said something that was all too evident at this point: "TRAIN!!!!"

As soon as I heard that, every sound vanished, and the train emerged, speeding past us at what looked like the speed of light. The train flew by our faces, inches away, with a woosh, woosh, woosh. I might have lost it if I had been a little more Jewish in the nose. Despite my worry, I felt a sense of serenity. I gazed through the train windows and saw shocked features of individuals on their way home, their minds plainly not prepared to have pubescent teenage eyes looking back at them from the darkness. I had become hypnotised by these folks, sitting there, commuting home, living their lives as they flew by, when the screeching of the brakes shook me out of my reverie. The train had come to a complete halt in the middle of the tunnel, and I could see the conductor leaning out of his window, his brain attempting to compute the information he was receiving, a bunch of teenage lads standing in a death trap from the front car.

During the pause, Donny straightened his back and yelled from the front of the line, "Run!" We ran.

A tragic event occurred here. When everyone turned around to sprint back out of the tunnel, guess who was now first in line? That's correct, Fat Ass. I ran as fast as my big ass could carry me, but it wasn't fair. I was trembling from the adrenaline, and a back draft from the train was still blowing into me. This was considered a "worst-case scenario."

I could hear my DJ screaming from behind me in the nameless darkness, "Run, you fat bitch, run!" I sprinted against the wind, the embarrassment, and my own body. That's how I ran. It seemed like a twisted, bizarre scenario from Stand by Me, except the sole lesson at the end was that marijuana outweighs life. As the light from the tunnel spilled out into the outside, I looked around to see Donny had hopped down onto the rails and was looking for something.

"Donny, what the fuck are you doing?" I inquired frantically.

"I dropped the weed!" he screamed back, as if it were obvious.

"Are you serious? You must leave immediately."

Donny looked at me as if I'd spoken the dumbest thing in the world. "Dude, it's weed."

I'm not going to argue. I leaned down and assisted Donny out of the tracks, but only after he had a bag in his hand. We went over the fence, trembling, and a few minutes later were crouched in a wooden play structure together, smoking quietly. We couldn't help but wonder what that little room looked like as the cannabis, terror, and adrenaline mixed together. I still wish we could have made it. The finest part of joining these guys was not just meeting friends, but also becoming a part of a world. Nobody knew about my secret life. My mother was initially content to let me go and stay out as late as I wanted because she was overjoyed that I'd found pals. Of course, my buddies and I were not studying knots for the Boy Scouts or assisting elderly people across the street. We were figuring out how to kick some ass. I got into my first alcoholic brawl. Everyone should own one. Everyone should get punched in the face at least once in their lives, in my opinion. It helps to shape character. Getting your ass kicked teaches you that your body isn't a fragile glass menagerie that can shatter at any time. You have to be clubbed together from time to time. Then you can heal and know you're fine. As a child, I was whopped. I'm wearing big leather belts on my naked ass. Screw it. My father used to drag me around by my ears and twist them when I talked shit, which I now see was terrible, not because of some physical abuse issue, but because I'm already Jewish with floppy-ass Dumbo ears, and for my father to tug on them was, well, anti-Semitic. Stupid Jew. But let me return to my original point. Getting punched in the face is beneficial. Unless you get pounded in the face too many times or too hard, at which point it ceases to be beneficial and mashes your brain into soup. However, getting your ass kicked is usually a good learning experience. And I was the professor this evening. Don't misunderstand me. This isn't some arrogant "I'm the man" declaration. I've been in a lot of fights, and I've lost the majority of them. But I won tonight, and it felt wonderful. To my credit, the motherfucker was babbling nonsense. It was late at night, and a group of us were drinking on the top field of Donny's primary school. Donny, DJ, and this kid Brian, whom you could never quite trust not to go violent, were all there. Some people only communicate through violence. Brian enjoyed striking. He wasn't a gangster, and he didn't have any weapons. He simply enjoyed striking. I was with Brian the first time I took nitrous oxide. Donny has known Brian since childhood. They'd gone to Camp Winnarainbow, the hippie camp run by that famed hippie clown Wavy Gravy. Brian was a Hessian with long hair. We all went to Safeway late one night, shoved whipped cream cans into our jeans, and strolled out beaming, anticipating the dessert party we were about to have. It's endearing to think of thirteen-year-olds getting high on something as innocent as whipped cream. It appears to be the ideal thirteen-year-old party drug. Get high and then have some hot chocolate.

They told me what to do later in Donny's room. "Crack it and suck it into your lungs," Brian continued, his eyes bright with enthusiasm. "Take as much as you can and hold it in." I followed the instructions. I yanked the plastic ring off the spigot and drew it toward me. The key to using whipped cream cans is to not shake them. When you shake it, you receive a mouthful of cream. I cracked it open and took a deep inhale. I held on to the surge of gas that filled my chest. Within two seconds, my brain began to rattle and quake, and the hippy crack kicked in. Nitrous oxide emits a noise. We used to call the wah wah wah wah sound you hear in your brain when nitrous hits the wah wah wah sound your brain cells make as they die. Your poor little brain's death knell, wondering what it ever did to injure you. So I sucked hard and listened to the symphony of death playing in my head the first time I puffed nitrous, and just as my mind began to mush and the bliss of the gas took over... bang! Brian, in his tenderness, struck me in the chest as hard as he could. When I reflect back on that night, I have no idea what he was doing or why he decided that was the best time to assault me. I recall not feeling anything and laughing for twenty minutes about it. So Brian was up on the top field, polishing his brass knuckles or munching gunpowder or whatever it is that such a person does. Donny, DJ, and a slew of other kids were also present. Gary, too. Gary was a jerk. At least, that's what we called him. I'm sure he's a lawyer, a postal worker, or a bank teller right now. I'm sure he's a family man who adores his two children, Castanella and Deflores. He's also a saint. Gary loved Deflores despite the fact that she was born with an additional brow. I'm sure he prays at night and gives to charity. I'm sure he never jerks off and considers all races equally. Gary, I'm sure, is incredible. But he'll always be a little bitch to me. And, like a b*tch, he said some nonsense that night. I'm not sure what. But I knew it was all too much for me, so I assaulted him. I rushed on top of Gary and began pummeling him for some inexplicable injustice. I struck him repeatedly. I punched him so many times that my sweater slid over my head and tangled me in it. So I removed it and continued pounding him. Then, from my left, Brian charged up and kicked Gary in the head with his steel-toed Hessian boots so hard I believed he killed him. It scared the crap out of me, but I suppose Brian's aggressiveness had its benefits as well. Allow him to strike you in the chest and kick your opponents in the head. To me, it seemed like a fair bargain. Gary, by the way, made it. He did not perish. We drank together later that night. I wrapped my arm around him and said, with sympathy well beyond my thirteen years, "It's okay, bro, no hard feelings, just don't act like such a bitch."


My exposure to this new drug-fueled consciousness was bringing me the kind of insight that I communicated to Gary. I went around, certain that I possessed some private information that had been hidden from the rest of the world's squares. I'd grin and nod my head as I passed a crusty old hippie or a Rastafarian-looking dude, as if to say, "Hello! Pot smokers are also present. "I understand!" There were a lot of puzzled looks, but I ignored them. My mother eventually saved enough money to get us our own house, and we moved next door to the King's X, a local hotspot for the worst characters imaginable. We had a metal bat that lived at our front door, and I can't tell you how many times I had to run outside with it and pound it on the ground to scare away some nasty mess pissing on my front door or some ugly trolls fucking in the weeds next to the home. People loved to pull up to the King's X and crank their motors for 45 minutes while blasting the latest Dr. Dre track at maximum volume without ripping through the space-time continuum. The bass shook the home, rattling the windows and keeping me awake at night. My mother was really fortunate to be deaf. What a jerk our landlords were to give her this house while failing to convey the decibel level her two hearing sons would be subjected to. We grew accustomed to it. My dilapidated house was approximately a mile from the Rockridge BART station, which served as my and my friends' home base. One kilometre. So far. I was overweight and lethargic, and I detested walking. I sagged over to the 59A bus stop and waited for it to arrive. I enjoyed hitchhiking. I'm not sure why, but every time I sat there, I'd raise my thumb and start asking folks whether they were coming my way. Do you think I could catch a ride?

Most folks gazed straight ahead as if deaf, so I would sign to them, "Can I get a ride?"

Back at Claremont, I walked the hallways with renewed vigour. The Jonos and Naomis of the world were no longer appealing. The black youngsters were no longer intimidating. This is especially true for the group's true gangsters. They got high, too, so we had some type of understanding and brotherhood, at least in my opinion. I, like all kids who start smoking marijuana, was enamoured with the pot imagery. I sketched pot leaves all over the place. The thought that this was incriminating never occurred to me because I assumed that only I and "my people" knew what a pot leaf looked like. I imagined those square bears would think I was obsessed with Canada. I recall drawing a large one on my folder for Portable Three, and when I pulled it out, a classmate leaned over, stole a glimpse, and whispered to her companion, "Damn, this white boy is crazy."

I beamed as my heart flooded with pride. "He certainly is," I thought. "He sure is."

It didn't bother me to be thought of as insane. At the very least, it drew me away from the faceless few white faces at Claremont. I was well-known. I was unique. Donny approached me at lunch with Jamie and DJ. "Meet us out by the BART parking lot after school, we have to show you something."

Jamie took a step closer and licked his lips. "It's a really good thing!"

I met the boys after school, and they spoke in quiet tones. We hurriedly retreated into a bush in the back of the BART parking lot that we had hollowed out. Joey was waiting for us inside. Joey only showed up when anything semi-serious was going on. At this point, he was too old and too connected to waste his time with juvenile stuff. This had to be significant. We were virtually hiding in the bush and could do the kinds of top-secret archcriminal things that are generally done in bushes.

Donny smiled and took a fistful of paper from his pocket. "This is—"

"Paper!" I just blurted it out.

DJ the brute gave me a threatening stare.

I turned pale. "Right, sorry, go ahead, Donny."

"It's white blotter acid." Donny appeared inebriated just handling the substance. "And it's the beginning of our empire."

I was perplexed. "Do we have an empire?"

Donny began ripping out acid hits one at a time.

He handed me one.

"The empire"—Donny pointed to his brow—"begins here." "Bring it to your tongue."

I followed instructions. I'd heard about acid before. My mother told me about her experiences in the 1960s as a young lady, how she ate acid and the world melted. It was supposed to be a cautionary tale, but all I could think during that chat was, "I'm gonna try that someday."

I guessed today was the day. Tuesday afternoon at three thirty was an ideal moment for a thirteen-year-old to experiment with acid.

"I once did acid with my grandpa, he had a pure LSD crystal in his office, and he handed it to me one day after I shot a deer," Jamie informed us. He licked it and urged me to do the same, and I was euphoric for a week."

We all rolled our eyes at the same time. Donny, who was always a little more spiritual than the rest of us, gave me a pep talk.

"You're gonna go places in your mind you never even knew were places, so don't fight it, just go with it." I swallowed my pill and began to wait for it to take effect. We sat around for a while, just talking and smoking, and I didn't feel much. Donny advised me to simply relax and wait. I suddenly felt a tickle in my stomach, similar to sickness but not as bad. Jamie was informed.

"That's it, man, it's on its way. That is strychnine."

Rat poison is strychnine. It is reported to have been mixed with LSD to make it more potent—the poison was seen as a type of hard-core badge of pride.

Jamie leaned in close. "It's rat poison, that's all it is." It amplifies the filth, but if you take too much, it might immobilise you."

Jamie was warned to quiet up by Donny.

"Don't listen to that nonsense. This is a completely white blotter. This is as clean as it gets. There's no strychnine, no nothing. Stop talking like that, guy, you're going to freak him out."

Jamie was unstoppable. "Also, try not to think about the impending nature of death or going insane." That's a sure method to never return from your journey."

"What do you mean, not make it back?"

"I spent two months in a forest after licking that crystal my grandfather gave me, convinced I was a bear, living on nothing but berries and moss." Only because my father formed a search team and rescued me did I make it back." Jamie's eyes were distant, and he began grunting like a bear.

"I know you're lying now." "Your father doesn't love you enough to look for you," Donny snarled at Jamie. He gave me a glance. "Let's have some fun. We have some business to attend to."

Me! Donny was going me to take care of business!

Donny and the boys were continually dealing with business, which is a broad term for "doing something that you don't need to know about."

We left Jamie and his warning tales behind and boarded the bus to Berkeley with Frohawk, the sewer dweller. Joey walked with us to the bus station and handed Donny a large bundle of cash right before we left.

"Don't fuck up," he told Donny before turning to face me. "And keep an eye on this kid, man, he's just about to jump into the deep end." Joey winked at me once more and walked away. We boarded the bus, and my mind began to warp into its journey. The rest of the world moved slowly behind me. The edges of my view woven themselves into a three-dimensional maze, and the patterns in the city's makeup showed themselves to me. I focused on a square inch of fabric on the bus seat, the intricacy of its stitching beckoning to me as it pulsed and pulsated like a clutch of worms. We stepped off the bus directly in front of UC Berkeley. This was around the moment my mind blew up. It seemed to me that none of the information being distributed in the lessons held in the buildings behind me was as important as the knowledge being leaked into, and out of, my mind by the ruptured pipeline in my brain. A system that had clearly been created to conceal this kind of understanding from me, lest the things I saw drive me insane. I was faintly aware that I was alone and that Donny and Frohawk had vanished; I just couldn't figure out why I should care. I was fairly certain that I cared about my mother. And she was going to be home in about five hours, so I knew I had to go see her. I walked four miles home from the UC Berkeley campus, mostly because I couldn't recall what a bus was. I arrived home and realized I'd left my house keys at home, so I sat on my front step for hours, looking at the inside of my eyelids, my head in my hands. By the time my mother arrived home, I'd gathered myself to the point where coherent ideas were once again feasible, so I basically spent the rest of the evening telling her how much I loved her and the different ramifications of the deeper meaning of love. Most parents would see this as a red flag, but for my mother, it was precisely what she had been hoping for, and it made her psychoanalyzed heart swell with pride. "He finally gets it!" she exclaimed. That was correct, I eventually did. My body ached when I finally came down, but my mind was sharper than it had ever been. I finally reconnected with Donny the next day at school.

"There you are, what the fuck happened to you yesterday?" I said. I felt enraged at having been abandoned, but I couldn't say for definite how or why this had occurred.

"We left you on the steps and went to handle some business," Donny said, laughing. You were gone when we returned. "How did you end up?" I let out a sigh. "I don't really know." I began consuming acid on a regular basis after that day. I'd take acid before gym class in the morning and float the rest of the day away. Morning classes were spent staring at my fingernails and the white roots of my nails as they looped around like fish in a tiny aquarium. The boys and I looked for each other during lunch since our faces were the only ones that appeared normal. We ate acid the same way we smoked marijuana. Every time. There were no psychedelic healing powwows. We dropped acid since we didn't have anything else to do. On acid, we never did anything cool. When Jim Morrison and the band went to the desert to eat peyote in the film The Doors, I thought to myself, "You can go places when you get high?" We'd drop acid and hang out at the subway station before going to class or writing graffiti. Psychedelic urbana. We pulled off white blotter slices and made our world more pleasurable. Blotter in white. Little white pages are shattering my thoughts. The disadvantage with mind-expanding drugs when you're thirteen is that there's not much to expand on.

"Did you ever notice canibus is spelled cani-BUS?" I asked Donny as I lay on his bed one night, the Cream Disraeli Gears cassette autoreversing to the beginning of the record for the sixteenth time.

"Fucking, we should start a cani-BUS where people could ride the bus normally but also smoke weed." "It's the CANI-BUS!" Donny was astounded by my business acumen. "Whoa. "Wait, isn't that cannabis?" I altered the topic. With the acid, we began to become legends. Joey and Donny had been impressed with the acid strain they had given me and had returned to the source to get many more sheets. I and the other guys were ready to transform our mental empire into a lot larger real-world drug empire. We set up business in Claremont, and word immediately spread. People recognized us and admired/feared us. The African drug traffickers were adamantly opposed to "that white boy acid." They let us market our stuff in peace because we weren't considered as direct competitors with them. Students from other schools would skip class to come buy blotter. Dysfunctional children from far areas like Berkeley and San Francisco would pack their donkeys and make the long journey to Oakland, where wise men offered enlightenment for three dollars a hit. Money poured in, and we lived like boy-kings. That is, until

Justin Sabbaro showed there and messed everything up with his pathetic heart.

# CHAPTER 6

# "THINGS DONE CHANGED"

One day, a fat seventh-grader approached us, eager to embrace a brave new world.

"Hello, I would like to purchase some LSD, please."

"Name?"

A anxious look around. A massive sweaty brow wipe. Nothing out of the ordinary here. We were exposing children to a perilous world.

"Justin Sabarro."

"Age?"

"Twelve."

"Perfect. LSD is a terrific mind-expanding drug that costs only three dollars; you won't find a better deal anywhere else. It sends you to another world, complete with drippy walls, profound concepts, and other foolishness. "Here you are, have fun!"

Justin inserted a dose into his lips, blissfully unaware. I didn't say anything to him, "Oh, and don't take LSD if you have a weak mind, dead parents, or a history of heart problems."

He lifted his head and clutched his chest. "Heart problems?"

I wish I had forewarned him in this manner. I didn't do it. Justin Sabarro ate the acid and completely ruined everything. Until that point, my mother had been desperate for information about how bad she suspected I was becoming. At home, things were in disarray, thanks in part to me. If mom had figured out what I was doing at school, she would have sounded the alarm much sooner, but thankfully, I was able to keep her away from that information for the most part. This was also because, due to apathy and financial limits, I was used as a conduit to communicate information to my deaf mother. Because Oakland Public Schools first refused to hire interpreters, I was given the unusual and tiny honor of attending and interpreting my own parent-teacher conferences. This was to be a pattern, and no matter how far down the ladder I crawled, it didn't seem far enough for the school system to pay for an interpreter. It took them years to recognize what I was doing and act on what should have been obvious. I also got really good at it. Not at translating, mind you, but at gradually changing the message I was receiving and conveying it to my mother in such a way that she never got the complete picture.

"Mrs. Kasher, your son has been truant an unacceptable amount of days this semester." The vice principal roared, hoping that my mother would hear some of it.

"Mrs. Kasher, while your son has not yet been truant an unacceptable number of days this semester, we are concerned that he does not make a pattern of it," I'd write.

I'd always reveal a portion of the truth, lest my mother merely grin and give the vice principal a thumbs up. She had to act concerned enough not to pique the teachers' interest, and they had to appear satisfied enough not to smack me. So her lip-reading eyes didn't pick up on anything, it had to look like what they'd said. It's a thin line to walk. I was an authority. My mother and I would frequently leave a conference discussing how odd the Claremont faculty was, how paranoid they were. Then there was Justin Sabarro, and I couldn't take it anymore. His arteries shattered the denial barriers I'd welded shut with lies. "How could I convey this message?" "This boy has a big heart." Very concerned! So madly in love that it really explodes... Oh, forget it; his heart exploded." I'd gotten fucked. Justin was a round-faced seventh-grader. At the time, white kids in the lower classes looked up to us as gods. We were a group of awful seventh graders. We were like a rumbling pack of greasers, but we were all black, so leather motorcycle jackets were out. School attendance was virtually optional at this point, and Donny and I and the boys had become more of a burden to the Claremont instructors than anything else. White scumbags, Mexican gangbangers, and black gangsters and crack traffickers. We'd done it. Officer Joe paid frequent visits to the school to fuck with us. This was done primarily to scare us and give the Claremont administration the idea that something was being done to address our concerns. He'd come into campus, approach us in the yard, and snub us.

"Hey, you assholes thinking about cutting class again?"

I detested him. "I was thinking about it, you know any good spots?"

"I'll be watching for you," he'd scoff.

"Are you pretending to be Dirty Harry or Charles Bronson right now?" It's quite convincing!" I had no idea when to quit talking. Everything changed dramatically when Justin messed everything up. The stakes were abruptly raised, and we were unprepared. Donny stopped me in the hall one day. "I'm screwed, man. "That kid Justin had a heart attack."

It was difficult to believe. This tiny scrap of paper had somehow short-circuited a child's delicate little cardiovascular system. This medication, which had taught me about the power of my mind, had taught him about the vulnerability of his heart. Anyway, there was no need to figure out how to believe it because Donny was standing in front of me, looking like he was having a heart attack. He was terrified.

I'd never seen Donny without a protective gangster cloak. Donny had always been the type of person who moved through life with ease. He appeared to be older than us all just because he was cool. People came to him for that reason, and they unknowingly worshiped him. It was primarily due to the fact that he was never afraid and always knew exactly what to do.

"I don't know what the fuck to do." He appeared to be terrified.

That's not good. Is that what he's asking? He's my go-to guy for situations like this. "Um. I'm not sure either, guy."

We were all a little fixated on stupid. Fortunately, Justin made our following step rather simple.

Nikki, a girl Donny had been seeing on and off for months, went to see Justin to see if he was okay.

"He tried to rape me!" she told us after the visit.

How about that, Justin? Weak in the heart, strong in the dick. That day, we paid Justin a visit. Whether he had a heart attack or not, he was beaten down by Donny while Jamie stood back, ranting about the Crips he would contact if this happened again. Justin then vanished from Claremont and from Oakland altogether. However, the Justin incident changed everything. Everyone's gaze was drawn to us right away. Overnight, we went from being invisible white lads to "those guys." Mrs. Hojo, the principal at Claremont, drew us in one by one to inquire about our relationship with Sir Justin the Weakhearted. After DJ had drooled all over her desk and Jamie had regaled her with stories of his youth in Guatemala shucking coca plants for his uncle Pablo, I walked in at the end of the questioning session. Jamie and I exchanged glances as he exited and I entered. The expression told it all: "Keep your fucking mouth shut." Easy. I'd spent my entire life lying to therapists. Principals were no problem.

"Hello, Mr. Kasher." She looked at me through a stereotypically principalish pair of horn-rimmed spectacles.

"Good day, Mr. Hojo... Mrs. Hojo, please accept my apologies... Sorry for my nervousness."

"It's fine. Take a deep breath, and then tell me everything you know about Justin Sabarro."

My plump cheeks turned rosy, and I appeared five years younger. "Is that the man who had a heart attack?"

Mrs. Hojo was not amused. "Yes, the boy. "Did you sell the LSD to him?"

"LSD? "Is that what the hippies drank at Woodstock?"

She was aware that she was being used. Her face was red-faced with rage. I'd won.

"You can leave now. I'll contact your mother about this."

I cracked a smile. "She's deaf, but would you like me to relay a message?"

"I'll call your grandmother then; just get out of my office."

As Donny took his seat in the questioning room, I winked at him. Maybe this was going to blow away after all. I was ambushed a few weeks later. My mother's home base was the UCSF Center on Deafness. A center dedicated to two of my mother's big passions: deaf equality and psychological diagnostics. Joy. I'd been in analysis for eight years at that point, and I was just thirteen. I was passed from analyst to analyst until I was in treatment eight times a week. Individual therapy, behavioral counseling, group therapy, and my mother's personal favorite, family therapy, are all options. Dr. Patty Susan, our family therapist, was a typical deaf fetishist. A newly graduated hearing therapist with a dual degree in deaf studies and psychology. People like this idolize the deaf. These are the people who stop you in the street to praise sign language, completely oblivious that you just signed, "The roast beef gave me twelve hours of explosive diarrhea."

Every week's appointment was basically an hour of Dr. Susan pointing out how much of a martyr my poor deaf mother was and how much of a jerk I was. To be honest, she was correct. I was a complete jerk. The more I plunged into my tiny universe, the more concrete my mother's lifelong worry of something wrong with me became. I had become the troubled child my mother had predicted I would be. Surprisingly, the worse I got, the further my mother delved into her own psychosis. My mother has always been a frenzied, emotional torrent. She used emotions as if they were weapons. Her shield was love, and her sword was guilt. The more I resisted, the more she tried to swallow me whole. She slept on my chest. She began weaving an emotional tether for me when I was old enough to no longer wear the real leash she tied around me when I was a baby.

I couldn't get through that one. It was formed from tough metal. She had a psychic connection to me that I couldn't shake. My mother would wake up the next morning with my absence palpable in her mind, vibrating like Spidey sense. She always seemed to know when I wasn't around. To be honest, I did leave a lot. Having a deaf mother makes getting out of the house a breeze. Actually, it wasn't so much sneaking as it was leaving in the middle of the night. If I wanted to, I could tramp, stomp, and break dance. Almost every night, I departed. Unfortunately, I would frequently sneak over to a friend's house, drink a little too much, and pass out. When I'd pass out drunk on DJ or Donny's couch, I could always bank on being startled awake around seven a.m. by desperate banging on the front door. I'd snap awake and groan as it dawned on me that my crazy mother had tracked me down. I'd stumble to the car with her, trying to ignore my predicament. My mother would reach over and pat my leg, appearing to reassure me that everything was fine but, in reality, patting me down for cigarettes or drugs. If she felt the hard square of a pack of cigarettes, she would clench her hand down, hard, on the pack in my pocket, attempting to snap my cigarettes in half. As we grappled and struggled, I'd pull away and scream in wrath, and the automobile would careen across lanes of traffic.

My mother's lunacy just added to my strong mistrust and animosity of all the other grownups around me. I was a venomous sphere. Of course, you could have cut that ball in half and viewed the fear's white-hot molten core. That was my main motivation. I didn't truly dislike them; I despised myself. I felt unimportant, shattered, and afraid. But I couldn't have told you that. All I knew was that I was furious. When I heard the intricate language of sorrow and dread emanating from within me, it perplexed me. I couldn't put it into words, and I couldn't convey it. It seemed like snarls and screams to me, so I spoke in that tone. Maybe I wasn't such a jerk after all. Maybe I just didn't know how to quit acting like one. I came at my weekly family therapy session with my mother, barely armed for war. That morning, I'd neglected to put on socks. Maybe if I'd remembered, I wouldn't have been locked up. I was unprepared for the run to the streets. Oh, those socks! When I walked into Dr. Susan's office, I realized something was wrong. Maybe I could just smell the cop's coffee breath in the office. This was not going to be your typical therapy session.

"So," Dr. Susan began, ignoring the large black cop in the room, "your mother told me you and your friends sold LSD to a boy who had a heart attack." "How did you feel about that?"

"Heartbroken?" I called her a model of kindness. "How should it affect me? I'm not sure, but it wasn't me who suffered a heart attack."

I could feel her set her clinical phasers to kill mode and gear up as her brow twitched.

"And have you taken LSD?"

This was the time for evasive maneuvers, but all I could think of was, "Me? No. No... I simply sell it. Er... sold it. It was something I used to sell."

"And do you take other drugs?" the excellent doctor said, unconvinced.

"No."

"So if I took a urine sample from you right now, it would be totally clean?"

As she stated this, the cop laughed, and I envisioned blasting his scalp and watching a brain composed of stuck-together donut holes fall to the floor. I made a rapid decision. "Okay... Maybe I've been in a car... do you know what hot boxing is? Who's smoking in the car? I may have been exposed that way."

Doc made a quicker decision. "So if we tested for LSD, then, that would be negative?"

"Look," I began, frantically searching my thoughts for something to throw the dogs off guard, "I've been in a car maybe... you know what forced dosing is?" Where hippies bind you with hemp rope and apply whetted LSD crystals on your lymph nodes and genitals as retaliation for bad business deals? I may have been exposed that way."

The cop laughed once more.

Dr. Susan shifted in her seat, bracing herself for the assassin's shot. "We can't even test for LSD, so thanks for the story." "Do you consume alcohol?"

The walls were closing in around me. This was clearly going somewhere...

"I mean, I have, you know, Passover, Bar Mitzvah, other Jewish stuff."

Dr. Susan scribbled furiously on her clipboard as she spoke. "Your mom told me you've been stealing from her, getting violent, cutting class, picking on retarded people?"

I was taken aback. "But I'm retarded!"

"She said you've been tagging on the walls inside your house?" She developed a gleeful confidence with each question she asked, as if she was finally living out one of her grad school role-playing fantasies.

"There's no way she can prove that was me," I shot back, realizing the pointlessness of the entire debate.

Dr. Susan laughed. "She saw you doing it."

"She's deaf!" I yelled back, desperate. You can't believe what she sees!"

The final blow.

"Here are your options. I propose that you be institutionalized for a few weeks. To have a safe place where you can be evaluated and prescribed appropriate medication."

She handed me some legal paper and a pen. "Here. I know it's difficult for you to say, so why don't you write your response? You type yes and drive there. Or type no and be restrained and transported there in an ambulance."

"FUCK YOU!" was the only thing to write.

I returned the paper to her.

She laughed. "I guess that's a yes then?"

I was subsequently taken to Ross Hospital, a teen psychiatric lockup facility. The ride there was nauseating and terrifying. A thousand doors slammed shut around my life every second. In the film Labyrinth, Jennifer Connelly takes a wrong step, walks through the wrong door, and ends up plummeting down an unending black hole. Hands cover the walls, thousands of bodiless hands slapping and brushing against her as she falls. These hands might aid her, they could stop her, but all they do is tickle her with the prospect of rescue. That's exactly how I felt. I was still free, but I was heading somewhere I knew I wouldn't be. My mother, who was supposed to be my protection, was right there with me. She was the one who was meant to put a stop to such activities. When my thoughts begged me to go to her, I was hit with the understanding, "Oh, that's right, she's the one sending you here."

The doors slammed closed behind me. I was lost in the maze.

One of the nicest aspects of being locked up in a mental hospital at the age of thirteen is... wait, I'm thinking.

When my mother left me in shock, I stared out on the foot-thick door that closed behind her. How on earth did I wind myself here?

For over an hour, I sat in the intake lounge, starring at that door, expecting it to fly open and a panicked young intake worker to jump in with a stack of papers, crying, "Mr. Kasher, Mr. Kasher!" I'm really sorry; we made a terrible error! You have no place here. What a weird lady your mother is, don't you think?"

We'd enjoy a cigarette and a cappuccino while laughing at women's lunacy and the world's injustices. Then I'd be let go and go get high. I continued to stare, but my intake worker never appeared. That night, I slept on a small hospital corner bed in a room devoid of sharp objects, shoelaces with which to hang myself, or anything remotely soothing. I awoke the next morning with the understanding and a nasty flood of memories of the fuckup chicken coop I was sleeping in. I blinked my eyes open.

FUCK.

I'm in a psychiatric institution.

I'm in a psychiatric institution.

I'm in a fucking mental institution.

A MENTAL HOSPITAL, to be precise.

HOSPITAL FOR MENTAL ILLNESS.

Fuck Fuck Fuck.

But there was no time to wallow in my rage because the mad house had a very strict schedule. Rounds began at 7 a.m., with an orderly knocking on your door and a firm, "Kasher, out of bed for showers!"

I walked out of my foam "safe slippers" into the corridor and smelled the fetid, chemical custard stench that pervades every hospital and institution. That smell recollection will never leave my nostrils. Every time I go to the doctor for an appointment, my nose takes me back to that corridor, where I stare down at my feet, wondering what happened.

When I arrived at the showers, I was given a meager towel and a hotel bar of soap. "Five minutes," said the orderly.

You know how a long, relaxing shower can make you feel calm and cleansed? That's not going to happen during the five-minute mental hospital shower. Even inside, you have a sense of institutionalization. I washed my hands and dreaded the rest of the day. The first activity was some sort of group ball game taught by the most upbeat counselor you could ever dream to vomit in the face of.

"This is FEELING BALL!" In contrast to the blackness coming from my heart, her disgusting glistening teeth shined dazzling white. "Put the emphasis on feeling!" When I throw the ball to you, tell me how you're feeling about your new mental health journey!"

With a big smile, the cheery little thing bounced the ball toward me. "Your turn!"

"What?" I couldn't believe I was doing this to myself.

"A feeling!" I wanted to rip her face off with my mind as she grinned.

"I feel like you are bad at your job." As my therapist's electric grin faded, I passed the ball to someone else.

"I'd suck your dick," the girl next to me said quietly.

I was flattered until I realized she was looking straight past me to her illusion a thousand yards away. I'd never gotten a blow job before, so the possibility of convincing this girl I was the lizard king and receiving a royal suck-off intrigued me. But, because there was a total lockdown after hours, there was little I could do with that offer other than jerk off to the memory of it well into adulthood. Crazy Dick is a jerk. The ball was thrown to the girl. She snarled at the cheerful little ball bouncer, "I feel like kicking your fucking teeth out." Oh, I guess I wasn't the only one. Dick Suck hissed at the cheerful little counselor and hurled the ball straight at her head, knocking her down. Alarms went off. Orderlies rushed in, not to exonerate me as in my vision, but to restrain my new companion and drag her into the quiet room. She foamed and kicked like a wild raccoon. Maybe I'll skip the blow job after all. Hello and welcome to the nut house. Have a good time. That night, one day down, I went to bed, not knowing when this would end.

The following few days were spent switching between groups, participating in a pitiful attempt at in-house schooling, and enduring hours upon hours of psychological testing.

They gave me 1,000-question personality tests, talk therapy sessions, role-playing, medicines, and Rorschach inkblot tests with inky outlines of individuals with fat bulges in their crotch and enormous busty chests, but if you indicated you saw she-males, you had "gender identity issues."(How unfair!)

I received a diagnosis. Oppositional defiant disorder, drug addict. Disorder of conduct. Clinical depression. Narcissistic, with ADHD, and "on his way to becoming a first-class sociopath." First-class. If you're going to be bad, you might as well do it in style.

There were meals, groups, games, meds, movies, levels, and points, as well as, of course, a padded cell. It's not all that horrible in there. Cool and smooth, and a location where you wonder how you ended up here. There were rambling teenagers with thick gauze wrapped around their wrists, abuse victims who couldn't return, covert drug addicts, and Jesus Christ. What about Jesus Christ? He was, indeed, present. At least, that's what one person said he was.

I could feel a fire of rage rising and blazing deep within my gut, attempting to escape. I'd been high for so long at this point that I hadn't felt that way in a long time. But, thanks to my 5150 and that bad weather, I have a two-week respite. The topical anesthetic I'd been dabbing at my life, Dr. Susan, was starting to wear off. I couldn't believe what they'd done to me or where they'd thrown me. I despised those fucking adults so much that I couldn't tolerate it. This therapeutic atmosphere did not appear to be therapeutic.

I couldn't believe how angry I was. And I believe I'd have been even outraged if I'd known then what I know now thanks to the benefit of 20/20 hindsight—that all of my therapists were correct. I wasn't angry; I was terrified. The fury was simply a layer of defense against the dread it masked. Sure, I despised those folks, but it was primarily because they symbolized something I was not. In command. Stable. Powerful. I wasn't any of those things. I remained enraged because what was behind that was too unpleasant. I was terrified. A terrified youngster.

Every day would end with a line of questions from one of the doctors.

"Are you ready to talk about your drug use or behavioral problems?"

"I'd really like to talk to you about that, but I don't have either of those issues." But I sincerely appreciate your thoughtfulness."

"Do you think your sarcasm is helping you get out of here sooner?"

His displeasure began to seep into his speech, cracking his therapeutic facade.

"I don't know, do you think the anger in your voice is helping you get through to me?" I gave a wide grin.

"You little prick." He'd snapped.

There was something incredibly rewarding about breaking through a therapist's professional armor. I'd hunt for a small chink, insert my little venomous prick, and begin pounding it till they lost their shit and I ejaculated victory all over them. I'd won when they lost. I felt so powerless, so at the mercy of these jerks most of the time, that stealing their authority felt euphoric. Unable to persuade me to participate in any form of talk therapy, they began randomly giving me drugs, one at a time, to see if they could get enough chemicals into my bloodstream to make me feel better. They only ever made me feel crazy. Zoloft, Ritalin, and Desipramine flooded my veins, scraped my bones, serrated my brain, and whirlpooled my concentration. Every second I was force-fed psychotropics, I swear to God, I could feel them practically tangibly in my body, affecting my chemistry, fucking my brain. I was on medication for years. That New Year's Eve, I went to bed at 10 p.m. Celebrating from my hospital bed, behind huge Plexiglas windows and walls, and around hospital corners, resolved never to return. Every second spent in that institution was a constant reminder that YOU ARE NOT NORMAL. At the same time, I found solace in that location. Nate was the only regular child there. He was an older teen, probably sixteen, and I thought he was as awesome as anyone I'd ever met. He and I would hang around in groups, making fun of the crazy people and discussing how much dope we were going to consume when we got home. I tried to wow him with stories about how much I got high, and I had no idea anyone was listening. I wasn't particularly intelligent, but I was heavily drugged at the time. He wasn't simply cool; he, like me, was pained by his life. We used to say hello to each other at night from across the walls of our kitty-cornered rooms. "Shave and a haircut," I'd say, and he'd reply, "two bits." I believe we did it to let each other know that there was someone else there who understood. I knocked one night and no one replied. Nate had vanished. He'd been let go. That night, I wept myself to sleep, hyperventilating and terrified, for no apparent reason. I recall crying as well when I got out. How fast you become institutionalised. After a two-week stay, I was ready to move in. Ready to be a thirty-year vet with my ass hanging out of a hospital gown performing the Thorazine shuffle and yelling about how the Tuesday pudding has arsenic in it because the Libyans are trying to murder me. Screw that. I escaped and returned to the true lunatic asylum, Oakland Public Schools. Since anyone could remember, my brother had been a straight-A student. He'd graduated from Claremont as an unblemished exemplary student and been offered a full scholarship to Oakland's best private college-prep high school, where he'd gone on to continue to get straight A's and, I assume, participate in fancy-lad sodomy parties where they wiped the cum off each other's chests with their paisley ascots.

My mother had been battling through school for years, desperate to become a deaf teacher. She pursued her master's degree as if it would define her and erase the mistakes she'd made in the past.

Dick the Dick, my grandfather, was an English professor at a nearby community college. Speaking about issues such as "Spousal Abuse: How to Do It!"

My grandma worked in the Oakland Public School System as a teacher. Without a doubt, I was laying the groundwork for a curriculum that would allow me to fail years later.

At the turn of the century, her mother was a teacher in Arizona.

Her mother's grandmother was a teacher in Utah in the 1800s, training Mormons to be creepily pleasant (yes, she came up with that!).

Her mother's mother's mother was in charge of training Abraham Lincoln when he was a child. (This is not correct!)

Her mother's mother's mother was Jesus' after-school tutor, quizzing him on topics such as "How to avoid the pull of Satan in the desert" and "Why the Jews seem cool now, but you should never trust them."

Her mother's mother's... well, you get the idea. My family placed a high priority on education.

So my failure to return to school, and, more troublingly, my refusal to care about the consequences, destroyed them. They were at a loss for what to do.

Fortunately for everyone, Dr. Patty Susan called my mother with an idea. What do you think? It was a shaky one!"Doctors at Ross Hospital apparently observed him repeatedly bragging to his friend Nate about how frequently he drinks and gets high with his friends Donny, DJ, and Jamie. I'm sending you some information about New Bridge, an outpatient rehabilitation program for adolescents in your area."

Mentally sick junior high school dropout in treatment is just slightly lower on the "you are going nowhere" list than mentally ill junior high school dropout. I was thirteen years old when I entered my first drug treatment. The Foundation for the New Bridge. A rehabilitation center for children!

New Bridge was administered by ex-cons and former junkies who, predictably, had a strange bedside style. On my first day at New Bridge, I was greeted by a terrifying man named Clarence, who delivered a soliloquy on "just what the fuck we are doing here."

So… What the hell are we doing here? The New Bridge Foundation is responsible for this. We are a resurrected New Bridge. Will you please accompany us across the bridge? There are several rules in New Bridge. This is a University of Arizona cup. You'll piss in it twice a week in front of me. This is my favorite aspect of my profession. I'm an ex-convict. I injected hundreds of thousands of dollars' worth of dope, borax, HIV, and hepatitis into my arms. I have steel veins and mercury blood. I've slain guys with my bare hands and bought prisoners for matchsticks. If you fuck with me, I'll treat you like a lovely cellmate.

Here, we will also learn arts and crafts. We'll learn how to manufacture stained glass and then chat about our emotions. Crossing your arms is a universal indication of being closed off and defensive. If you're defensive and closed off, I'll punch you in the gut as hard as I can.

I'm not sure it went exactly like that, but that's what I remember. The stained glass, on the other hand, was real. For whatever inexplicable reason, we would spend hours processing emotions and being shouted at before retiring to a basement to solder glass. I'm not sure what the therapeutic value of that was, but I recall soldering a glass imitation of a spray can and feeling pretty proud of myself.

"You need to get rid of your using friends," a common refrain in rehab. You require fresh playmates, as well as new playgrounds and playthings."

Of course, the premise is that until a person quits his drug-based social unit, he has little chance of being sober. It makes sense and is rational. Unfortunately, it's also the most ridiculous expectation to ask of a teenager who is high and fucking up because he despises everyone but his friends. My friends were the only people I had. Getting high with Donny, Joey, DJ, Jamie, Corey, and all of those fuckups was the only thing I enjoyed in my life. And these fucking adult ex-cons were scaring me and telling me to get rid of them? And what are you going to do? How do you make stained glass? That's right. More to the point, I was entirely skeptical that I had a drug problem at the time. What I had was an issue with grownups having an issue with my medicines. For me, narcotics were the answer to my difficulties. Remember how I used to feel alone, embarrassed, and broken? Those feelings were alleviated by drugs and my buddies. Anyway, I could have quit whenever I wanted; I just didn't want to. One of the positive aspects of New Bridge was that they persuaded my mother and grandma to put my "recovery" ahead of getting me back into school. One of the negative aspects of New Bridge was that my "recovery" interfered with my "drug use." I had to piss in a small cup near to Clarence's ravenous eyes twice a week on odd days. This compelled me to think of novel methods to leave the world behind. Leotis, the semi-homeless buccaneer, had gone to rehab a thousand times and knew exactly what I was in for. "Those fucking piss tests make it nearly impossible to smoke weed for any length of time without getting caught." You must exercise caution." This was correct. Pot, more than any other substance, keeps itself in your system and accumulates over time as you smoke more. You may pass the test once or twice, but you will eventually be detected. That didn't stop many from attempting it. No one, and I mean no one, was attempting to be sober at New Bridge. We were all just figuring out how to pass urine tests. We sipped teas and cranberry juices and tried to wash the THC out of our veins with water while the kids ate niacin to flush their systems. I once drank a quart of vinegar, which seared my insides and caused me to vomit acidic poison. However, I passed my drug test! I obtained a pass-guaranteed tea the second time, drank it, and failed. I had to eventually resort to drinking and eating acid, snorting speed, sucking down nitrous, and eating mushrooms. Life in rehab is quite difficult. I despised New Bridge, but I also adored it. I encountered youngsters who were so unacceptably bad to everyone that they were taken off to be fixed. Every day, I'd ride the bus up to New Bridge, and they'd try to make me talk about how I felt. I didn't mind; I was used to being scrutinized. But, just behind that callousness, I detected a shift in the air. I hadn't left the psychiatric hospital. I had not yet left Claremont. That turmoil had not left me; it was still all over me. The childhood suspicion that something was seriously wrong with me was manifesting itself in these gatherings. What kind of thirteen-year-old attends rehabilitation? I couldn't express my shame, so I did what I always do when I'm overwhelmed: I acted like an asshole. I'd cross my arms and make fun of everyone. I was talking so much nonsense that the other kids told me to shut up. When fellow drug-addicted adolescents in recovery urge you to cool out, you know you're an asshole. But they liked me as well. I was expressing their thoughts.

FUCK THIS LOCATION.

"Fuck this place!" During family group, I'd yell across the room. My mother's sign language interpreter strained to keep up with my rage. Health insurance was able to pay for translators more easily than Oakland Public Schools. The interpreter, on the other hand, didn't appear to be overjoyed at the prospect of interpreting for a real-life teenage jerk. I was furious.

A new counselor, fresh from university, had begun work at New Bridge that night and seemed set on fucking with me.

"Hello, everyone. My name is Tim Hammock, and I'll be in charge of the adolescent groups here from now on." I'm quite pleased about my new work and some of the changes I intend to introduce here in the near future. We have some kids who I believe want to change and some who want to help. And we have those kids who are really just here to be speed bumps on the route to recovery for someone else."

Tim fixed his gaze on me. I gave him a kiss.

I'd been caught coming to a party with a youngster named Mateo from New Bridge who was old enough to drive and another, much stupider boy in rehab named Thor.

Thor was named after the Norse god who carried a massive hammer, but our Thor appeared to have been battered in the head with a real hammer.

Mateo and I dropped Thor off the previous weekend after we had all been drinking. Later that night, he stole his father's car and, while stopped at a red light, saw a police cruiser go by. Even though they were driving straight past him without looking back, Thor's small fish brain was convinced they were going to arrest him. He sped past the red light as quickly as he could. As they flipped their car around and activated the siren, the cops probably high-fived themselves for making such an easy arrest.

Thor led them on a high-speed chase that culminated with him crashing into someone's living room, jumping out of the car, and continuing the chase on foot. Thor isn't that bright.

Tim sat back in his seat and leaned forward. "Thor has made some bad decisions in the last week, and he is aware of it." But after speaking with him, I'm confident he wants to change, and Thor has agreed to empty his contracts here, on a group level, to prove it to us all."

Emptying your contracts is rehab jargon for snitching on all of your buddies. Tim had persuaded him to spill all the dirt he knew about the other people in the rehab in order to avoid the lengthy jail sentence he was sure to face. This not only served as a sick proof of sincerity, but it also rattled the group and brought all the secrets and dirt to the surface. There was a lot of filth around. Gerald was gay, Claire kissed the spot in the bathroom where Mateo's dick and balls touched during group, Pablo was flirting with the ex-whore receptionist, and I went to that ecstasy party where we were all high. After Thor's confessional and everyone's secrets were revealed, I shouted, "Fuck this place!" and glared at Tim. "And fuck you for using Thor's stupid ass to bust us."

Thor awoke from his dumb trance. "Did you just call me stupid?"

My gaze was drawn to Thor's massive girth. Yikes. "Of course not," I replied. That is not something I would do."

Thor smiled and nodded, pleased with himself. My mother had become a kind of model rehab parent, constantly involved and completely oblivious to the fact that her own dysfunctions were at least part of the problem, as she was at every group, every counseling session, closely following as the interpreter translated my raging stream of obscenities. I was continually humiliating her. The tables had shifted. I was humiliated as a child by how she said things; now she was humiliated by what I said.

"This is a fucking joke!" You catch us doing things we're going to do regardless." I locked my gaze on Tim. "Do you just enjoy being a dick because you are an adult?"

Tim reacted angrily, "Do you enjoy wasting everyone's time here?" What's getting in the way of the youngsters that want to improve here?"

"No one wants to improve here!" Can't you see that, you stupid ass? We're all imprisoned here like little rodents. We're all eager to get high. Most of us are already!"

Oops. There is far too much information.

"Like who?" Tim inquired, hungry.

"Well, like your mother and I smoked some rocks together before I bent her over the soldering equipment." Perhaps I'd gone too far. Tim's face became enraged, and I feared he was going to hit me. I enjoyed irritating adults. My mother intervened at this time, speaking through her interpreter, who was already flustered and fucking up every fifth word. "Why don't you hug some respect?" he'd suggest.

"Have. Have some dignity." I was teasing him, scolding him, interpreting for my mother, and participating in the group discussion all at the same time. Everyone liked to comment about what a jerk I was, but no one mentioned the communication whiz I was becoming.

"Don't blame Tim for catching you doing something wrong," my mother replied.

I let out a sigh. "I'm doing something incorrect. There was no error. Wrong. You're making her sound like Frankenstein, dude."

"Right, sorry." The agitated little interpreter didn't seem grateful for the public corrections I was assisting him with.

"It's time for you to take responsibility for your own acting."

"Actions! IT'S THE ACTIONS. Jesus. "You"—I turned to face the interpreter—"return to interpreting school." Mom, please leave me alone. Go fuck yourself, the rest of you."

It was requested that I depart New Bridge. Tim kissed me goodbye. What a jerk.

# CHAPTER 7

## "SORTA LIKE A PSYCHO"

With my first term at "recovery" completed and the Claremont monkey off my back, I figured I was in for a fantastic summer. Unfortunately, my mother was not as enthusiastic as I was.

When I got home the next night, she was sobbing at the dinner table. When I stepped in, she glanced up and began sobbing. "What did I do to make you like this?" she asked, signing her name.

Oh my God. This type of discourse was becoming more common, and I couldn't stand it any longer.

"I make every effort to assist you in changing. I just keep hoping that you'll improve and become a better person. But I'm beginning to believe you'll be this way forever. I'm curious whether I made you like this. I sometimes wonder what you'd be like if I wasn't deaf."

My mother looked up at me with a pathetic expression on her face that I will never forget. I recall thinking, "She doesn't realize how helpless she really is." Nothing she does or says will ever change my mind. "I'm not malleable." I approached her and sat in the chair next to her. I took her hand in mine. I tried to be concerned. I tried to be human once more. I looked at the books mom had stacked up on the kitchen table around her: The Difficult Child, Tough Love, Parenting a Child with ADD, and dozens more whose names alluded to the theme of my household: I was broken, and that was the sole topic of discourse.

I despised my mother's sobbing. I adored her. But it never occurred to me, not even for a second, to change for her. I merely thought she was insane for crying over me. Perhaps first-class sociopath wasn't too far off after all. We sat there silently for a time, she trying to forgive herself, me attempting to blame myself. I eventually got up and left her to cry. That nonsense was too much for me. I pretended I didn't care, but all I wanted to do at the time was get fucked up and delete myself, obliterate the memory of my mother's weeping. That's exactly what I did. I wanted to be free of those memories. Perhaps that is a kissing cousin of caring. I became high and forgot. I got high and stealthily strengthened another paper-thin membrane wall around my emotions. I'd feel much worse the following time. That was all I ever want. I didn't want to be happy. I just wanted to feel nothing. Who would want to sense anything like this going on around them? I needed to get out, and luckily for me, there was a trapdoor into oblivion at the bottom of every forty-ounce bottle of malt liquor. I dashed in and checked out. My mom informed me of my summer plans the next day. "Things are about to change." I can't keep allowing you to exert power over me and my family. Larry is also going insane."

"Fuck Larry."

My mother's pupils constricted. "I've been trying, but having you in the house kills the mood."

I pretended to vomit all over the kitchen. Larry is in a bad way. Larry had been my mother's boyfriend for a long time. The poor wuss. He hadn't agreed to be my stepfather and, unlike others, tried his damnedest to get out of my way. That was almost impossible for me. Larry was a Ph.D. student in entomology at the University of California, Berkeley. Ward, my mother's ex-boyfriend, who used to enjoy nothing more than flinging us around the room to assert his control, was nerdy, shy, and amusing. Larry simply sat back and read nerd classics like The Lord of the Rings, The Hitchhiker's Guide to the Galaxy, and The Principles of Pesticide Alternatives in the Controlling of Northern California Aphid Populations. My mother had finally discovered her beta man after much seeking. He was pleased to sit back and watch while a little deaf pussy was bequeathed to him. I couldn't even allow him to do that. Cool or not, he was still an adult, and I despised him even though he was quite pleasant. I irritated him so much one day by continuously waking him up with my screaming battles with my mother that he screamed, "FUCK YOU!" Larry developed some nuts! I was blown away. In any case, my craziness had strained their relationship to the breaking point, and it would very certainly have been severed had I been allowed to spend the entire day at home, no school, no rehab. My mother had different plans.

"This is a legal document. I'm going to tell you about your educational options, and then you're going to sign it and commit to return to school this summer. If you don't, I'm going to send you away."

If you started screwing up at Oakland Public Schools, there were a few of distinct paths you might go. There were continuation schools, which were similar to regular schools if someone had had a bad life and been sent to prison, and special ed schools, which were similar to regular schools if they had had a schizoid break and gone insane.

By the time I dropped out, Oakland Public Schools had had about enough of me. Between the never-ending fights, the continual class cutting, the never-ending pot smoking, and the general malaise of awful behavioral problems, I'd been labeled as more of a nuisance than anything else. I became a problem rather than a student, and a massive crack beneath me opened up large enough for me to fall into. I dropped out of junior high when Peter Cooke beat me up, and unbeknownst to me, that was another trapdoor that opened up behind me and sank me deeper into insanity. I became disoriented in the system.

My mother and grandmother, most likely because of the professional, therapeutic prism through which they saw the world, chose to send me down the path of the insane rather than the criminal. But, at that age, the difference is fairly negligible. Then then, it may be at any age.

I was told that I had failed eighth grade and that if I didn't want to repeat junior high, I needed to spend some time at a school that could help me bridge some of the academic credit deficits I had accumulated. I consented to one of the greatest bait-and-switch jobs of all time.

The small yellow bus arrived the next day to pick me up and transport me to school.

The adolescent's lowest mode of transportation is the short yellow bus. It's the retard bus, a mode of transportation for children who can't walk, talk, or think. I got red when I saw that monstrosity pull up in front of my house. I stared at my mother as if to say, "You have to be kidding me."

She just said, "Go," and pointed to the bus. My self-esteem dropped 50 points the moment I stepped onboard and was greeted by thick-browed paste eaters waving cheerfully, "Hello, mister!" Kill me right now. I'd remain a virgin for the rest of my life if this information got out to my friends. The bloody short yellow bus! Do you realize how difficult it is to meet girls while riding the small yellow bus? It's difficult. You must remove their headgear. You must persuade the girl that your penis is made of candy. You must bribe the bus driver to turn away. I'm joking!

I had accepted to attend a school called The Seneca Center for the Severely Emotionally Disturbed Youngster without fully comprehending what I was getting myself into. Something was off the moment I walked in. Thick security doors slid open and autolocked behind me. Fortified school entrances are never a good indication. I took a look around. This was not like any other school I'd ever attended. Adults stood vigil at each of the one main classroom's entry and departure points, their eyes darting back and forth at the pupils, waiting for something, anything, to happen. As soon as you went inside, you had the impression that anything could happen. You can tell when you're in a room with folks who are out of control. When you share the air with the mad, you can taste their tinny chemical garbage. The teacher went on as if this wasn't a cuckoo's nest and she was just teaching a regular class, not these crazy youngsters. Meanwhile, the kids were muttering and ripping out their hair. Students gazed up at me with malicious grins that I misinterpreted as "I'll whoop your ass, white boy," rather than "I'll eat your ass after disemboweling you, white boy," which was new to me. People rocked back and forth or laughed at unspoken jokes. These were the kids who made their gangmates uncomfortable with their degree of brutality. I surveyed the room for familiar faces. There were only a few. Ray, one of the kids, grinned at me. He was a gorilla of a boy, simply gigantic, and as wonderful an ally as I could wish for here. I returned her smile. When you work in therapeutic settings like this, you become good at scanning a room and tasting its energy to determine what role you will play in each situation. In certain places, such as New Bridge, I'd soon become the loudmouth clown, gaining popularity by making people laugh. In some places,

I'd become quiet and try to blend in. Seneca Center for the Severely Emotionally Disturbed Child was one such facility. "Keep your fucking head down," I instructed myself. I found a seat. Within seconds, a boy named Jonathan, who had been sharpening his pencil with zeal, leaped at another pupil and attempted to thrust the pencil into his neck, presumably to impress the new kid. He hadn't even started swinging when security pounced on him and dragged him, foaming and kicking, into the built-in padded cell at the back of the classroom. Four enormous men threw that boy into the "quiet room," forcefully, without even registering an emotional reaction to their rage. For the rest of the period, Jonathan screamed freaking murder. The irony of the silent chamber is that by the time you get there, you are anything but quiet. Another nonsense clinical phrase. It was a padded fucking cell, not a quiet chamber. A padded cell right in the middle of class! What a time saver. What the fuck was I doing? Nothing distracts me more from a lesson about the Nia, Pinta, and Santa Maria than the low, deep thudding of a highly mentally disturbed youngster's skull continually banging against an improperly padded cell door. I believe that child was abandoned. Following the attempted murder, a Mexican child leaned in and shouted, "What you claimin', fool?" He was effectively asking me which gang I belonged to. "I'm from Oakland, man, we don't gangbang!" I puffed myself up and responded. The Mexican child looked at me with menacing eyes for a beat before nodding and turning away. I pretended to be tough as I emptied my bowels. The recess bell rung. Everyone queued up in twos, like a military operation—no, more like a jail routine. I looked down the line; everyone was already paired up, with established relationships. Finally, the recess bell rang. As we were allowed, two by two, out onto the yard to essentially just get some air and do laps around the yard, the kids raised their hands to show that they weren't carrying anything. It was as if they were preparing us to be the inmates they expected us to be. Except for Ray, everyone had a yard pal. He grinned and motioned for me to join him on the platform. Uh-oh. So, here at the Stab, let me get things straight. You in the Neck Academy, the place teeming with the worst of the worst baby Hannibal Lecters, are one boy twice your size with no pals and a large toothy grin calling me to stand with him? I'd never been raped and murdered before, and it sounded awful. I was about to shout "My appendix!" or "My anal virginity!" since I knew I was about to be killed like one of Lenny's pets in Of Mice and Men when one of the Gestapo guards yelled at me, "Kasher, line up!"

Yes, sir!

I swallowed hard and accepted my fate. Hello, terrible world!

I scooted over to Ray and smiled feebly. He returned the smile. He didn't say anything. Neither did I. I cried out. As he turned to smile at me, I could feel his broad grin. Foreplay? He presented me with a little notebook. I looked down and read, expecting to hear something like, "We can do this gently or rough."

"My name is Ray," the note said. "I am deaf."

I inhaled again as relief flooded my pores. I giggled as I threw my head back. Ray's brow furrowed in rage, thinking I was laughing at him. When I signed, "No no, don't hit me!" he had cocked his fist to terminate my life. I'm just glad there's a deaf kid here!"

Ray gave me a wide smile and shook my shoulder.

"You deaf?" he asked, his eyes detecting my fluency in signing.

"No, my mother, father deaf."

He smiled once more.

"Mother, father deaf" is how individuals like myself introduce ourselves to deaf people, the simple grammar serving as a kind of introduction into deaf society. It's a membership card to an extremely exclusive club. Regular hearing people can spend their entire careers working in the deaf world, establishing themselves as great allies to the deaf community, and being respected by all, yet they will always remain "hearing" and "other."

A child with deaf parents, however, who signs "mother, father deaf," is readily recognized as a member of the family. We're not hearing anything. We are the unusual exception to the rule, hearing individuals who are trusted as insiders in a society that is intrinsically suspicious of hearing people. Is it possible to blame them? Consider how you would address a deaf person if you met one on the street. Consider your slow-talking, buffoonish gesture disdain... Do you want to talk to me now?

This was, in any case, a good thing. My nuthouse school pal was the biggest guy in this mad quagmire who was alone because no one understood how to talk to him. This was welcome news. Ray had been placed in Seneca for a similar reason to mine—no one knew what to do with him. He was the only deaf student in a local school district, and as the lone bruised fruit, he was left to wither on the vine. He didn't get anyone's attention until he started destroying the other fruits. He smashed enough to be labeled "severely emotionally disturbed" and fell through his own trapdoor. Everyone around me was trapped in the same way. Stuck in the system's filthy cogs. Trapped in the first of what seemed like an endless series of institutions.

Without a doubt, some of these youngsters were doomed, their heads fried by drugs or beatings or simply biology playing a trick on them, flooding their brains with crazy-guy chemicals. Most, however, were like me, kids who took a soft left turn and didn't realize they were heading into no-man's land until they were so far gone that when they looked back, they realized they had no idea how to get back. They were suffocated. They had gone astray. I was surrounded by lost boys. I, too, was befuddled.

If we ever spoke out of turn, even if it was just one word, we had to stand for five minutes with our noses against the wall. Standing there, my nose brushing the coolness of the concrete pylon in front of me, I thought, "If you weren't severely emotionally disturbed when you got here, you sure would be by the time the bell rang to go home."

When it came time to leave, I said my goodbyes to Ray and boarded the fucking yellow bus. As a seriously crippled wheelchair-bound passenger shouted in hopeless agony at her damaged body, her broken head, I collapsed into my seat. Here was my new school life, framed by horrors. All I wanted was to be okay. I didn't feel anything like that.

I persuaded my driver to put me off a half-block away from my house so that the neighborhood boys wouldn't see me getting off the tiny bus. I returned home, smoked a joint, and reconsidered. I needed to get the FUCK out of there, and the only way I could do that was to be an absolute angel every single day. I'd never make a sound, and I'd never say anything clever. Make yourself unnoticeable.

I didn't say anything. I remained in Ray's clutches. Months had gone. For the time being, my acute emotional disturbance has been arrested. Every day at Seneca, I realized that if Hell existed, here is where the young people who lived there went to school.

I managed to straighten up enough to scramble and fill out a feverish application to Maybeck High School. It was renowned as a hippy school where "creative thinkers" went. I was hoping "creative thinkers" meant "slightly severely emotionally disturbed." I managed to put all of my cerebral resources into this program and create something spectacular.

It was a private school that my family couldn't afford, but I had a hunch it was the only place that would look at my inability to graduate from junior high as a result of being intellectually understimulated, rather than being busy selling drugs.

I submitted an application that included a personal statement as well as a comical hard-luck story about my life that tugged at your heartstrings, similar to the book you are presently reading.

It was successful. They not only got me in, but they worked out an arrangement with my mother in which she would pay a pittance, I would work in their office twice a week, and we would be able to keep me in that school. When I received the admission letter, I proudly displayed it to my mother and grandma, as if it finally validated me as an intelligent human being rather than a psychological equation to be solved. My mother and grandmother were overjoyed. I felt like I'd been granted a fresh start, a blank slate.

That night, DJ, Donny, and I smoked a joint in celebration.

"Here's to me never going back to that fucking Seneca Center."

I was experiencing an unusual sensation. Optimism?

"I just got to get through this school, man. I can't screw this up." I really meant it.

Donny gave me a glance. "You'll have to wait to get high till the weekends then."

I glanced at him as if he'd just spoken Cantonese to me.

"I'm not kidding, man. "I discovered it at Kaiser," he explained.

Donny had lately been admitted to the Kaiser Chemical Dependency Program.

"Didn't they say you could get high on weekends?" What the heck, your rehab sounds fantastic!"

"No, fool, they didn't tell me that, it was something I figured out," he said. "The first two things they tell you in recovery are the things you're not going to do. Get rid of your pals and quit getting ripped off? No one is going to do that, but you have to see through the message, guy. There's no place for anything else at the rate we're going up. So, if you want to succeed in school, just wait till Friday to get high and you'll be OK."

It made sense in some ways. It was strange, though, that I was getting this counsel from Donny, the largest marijuana smoker I knew.

"But don't you get high every day?"

"Yeah, and have you noticed my school career going well?" Donny stated unequivocally. It was a good point; he was in almost as much trouble as I was and had recently been expelled from St. Mary's, a private Catholic school.

I decided to consider Donny's idea. I had created my opportunity to pull myself out of this small slump I was in. It didn't make sense to me that I would fail in school. I knew I had a sharp mind on some level. My entire family was intelligent. I was the one who screwed up. The source of all troubles. The so-called "identified patient." I'd show it to everyone. I'd start this school and start fresh. Not exactly sober, but at least reasonable. From Monday to Friday, I'm not getting high. I wanted this more than I had ever desired anything before. My arithmetic teacher had a hand malformation that left him with only his thumbs on my first day, as if to reaffirm that I was in the proper place. So the first thing I saw when I went in was his two big thumbs up. Way, way up! I opted to see this as a good omen. Maybeck was fantastic. For the first time in my life, I was being challenged. There were several attractive women looking at me. I could invite Donny and DJ to a social scene, which made me valuable to them. It was a wonderful four months. Around the one-month mark, I was sitting in the park after school when a youngster called Jonah smoked a joint.

"Let's smoke," he suggested.

"No, I can't." I can't smoke throughout the week or I'll go insane. If I smoke now, I'll never finish my assignment."

"Oh, come on, smoke now, you'll be able to clear your head by six and then do your homework." That's exactly what I'm doing."

Oh, yes! It all made clear now. Smoke first, then get to work! At six. Do the work at six o'clock. Work begins at six o'clock. Six. Six. Six. Six. 666.

I snatched the joint. Oblivion. Of course, at six o'clock in the morning, I was sitting in a bush with Donny, smoking and sipping Maybeck. Three months later, I was failing out of school and was officially kicked out following a physical altercation with our flamboyantly gay acting teacher. (Is there another type?)

I'd been sacked from the school production of Our Town for constantly missing rehearsals and making fun of our teacher's ridiculously stereotyped "lithp."

I was on academic probation, and I didn't think I'd make it to the conclusion of the semester anyway. I was abruptly removed from the production and replaced by a jerk from the grade above me. There was no charisma, no flair, just enough etiquette to win over "Our Lady of the Stage."

I stormed into the theater on opening night, rooted my way backstage, eager to give the cast a good-luck hug. Instead, I was met by my flamboyant adversary.

"Who thaid you could be back here?"

"It has been stated. I'm just dropping by to wish the cast luck."

"Thorry, no thanks."

"I apologize. But you included the th, thanks. Don't be a jerk, let me just say hello."

I went to scoot past him and realized he was a fucking dude, lisp or no lisp. He shoved me up against the wall, smashing my head against it and jolting me awake. I began yelling every obscenity I knew at him. "Get your FUCKING hands off of me, you fat failure." I'm going to cut your throat."

He laughed. "It's pronounced thlit your throat." He hurled me outdoors onto the sidewalk.

"You couldn't think of a more original high school production than Our Town?" I cried feebly into the concrete.

The next day, I was fired. I was perplexed. I'd really wanted to go to Maybeck. If you had presented me with two doors, a la Let's Make a Deal, and said flatly, "Behind door number one is success at Maybeck, the ability to make it through school, and feel good about yourself." "You guessed it: a bag of weed and a forty-ounce bottle of malt liquor," I would have chuckled at the silliness of the option. Without a doubt, I desired Maybeck more than I desired to get high. But, unbeknownst to me, I had already passed a small invisible border. Yet another fork along the way. I'd reached a point where desire had little or no bearing on whether or not I drank and got high. I was obeying the call of the monkey on my back, not engaging in a fight of wills. I had lost control and had no idea what had happened. Of course, I wanted to get through that school more than I wanted to get high, but here I was, high as fuck and kicked out. I couldn't figure out how I'd managed to outpace my own head. For a few weeks, I returned to Maybeck. My new, exciting social life was there, as were the individuals I got high with. I couldn't bear the thought of letting it go. Every day, I'd take the bus to Berkeley and meet Donny around midday to smoke with kids at The Grove, a eucalyptus forest near the UC Berkeley campus. We'd show up, say hello casually, and then sit down to get down to business of getting high. I kept showing up, unable to understand that I had to let go of the idea of that school and accept who I had become: a fucking fourteen-year-old failure. I showed there one day, weeks after I'd been kicked out, and was rounding the bend into the grove when I overheard my schoolmates discussing me. I crouched behind a bush and listened, quivering with embarrassment and trembling with pain.

"It's sort of pathetic that he continues showing up here, man. I mean, hello, you no longer attend school here."

Jonah, the same fucking kid who pushed me to get high when I was six, was now criticizing me?

Olivia, a girl I'd had a crush on, chuckled and agreed. "I mean, he never went to school here, did he?" Technically, yes, but he was actually only here to get high. We'd best get a smoke in before he comes over and begins mooching off of us again."

They both laughed. I was about to cry. I never returned to Maybeck after that. I rode the bus back to Oakland, unsure of what I was going to do next. I was wondering what the fuck was wrong with me, if I'd ever be okay. Screw it. I'd find a friend, a forty-year-old, and a way out of my head. That night, Donny and I drank Crazy Horse and laughed about everything. Everything was amusing. Everything is a shambles. Fuck the entire universe. Jamie the liar had been missing for weeks. He reappeared one day, battered and bruised. He was speaking with a Mexican accent. This was novel.

"I've been in prison, Holmes. I've been getting into some serious gangster shit. "I'm a Norteno now," Jamie said, pulling out a red rag and waving it in front of us like a matador.

The Nortenos are a Mexican street gang in Northern California that has a long history of rivalry with their southern counterparts, the Surenos. Jamie's claim of going to prison and joining the gang was, to put it mildly, difficult to believe.

Miguel, Jamie's new friend, perplexed our skepticism. Miguel was a terrifying-looking Mexican kid dressed head to toe in Norteno reds. He was the genuine article. Miguel was a gangbanger from West Berkeley, a notorious Norteno neighborhood. He was a foot taller than the rest of us and weighed at least 250 pounds. He was tough and intimidating, but there was something strange about him. Miguel muttered to himself and laughed at the end of his own sentences, having barely made a joke. It was unsettling, but we were relieved to have him around; when would we get to hang out with a real live Mexican gang-banger again? Miguel resembled a cartoon character of a sly weasel who was sent to prison and gained fifty pounds by lifting weights in the yard. When he looked at you, you couldn't be sure you weren't going to have to defend yourself from being eaten alive. Miguel was one of the strangest and most off-kilter people I'd ever met, and Jamie loved to show him off like a prize buck he'd shot while hunting.

"Have you met my carnal, Miguel?"" he'd say. "My true Norteno hermano!""

We'd all roll our eyes and then look anxiously at Miguel for some kind of reaction that would explain the two of them's social dynamic. Jamie had done something real? Was this some bizarre, long-form practical joke?

Unfortunately, all Miguel ever did was chuckle and shake his head at Jamie, as if he were the cutest thing ever. Miguel eventually stopped being an exotic social anomaly and simply became one of the boys. A genuine gangbanger! We were overjoyed.

I was even more proud of the day I faced Miguel. Normally, a six-foot-tall, 250-pound gangbanger would be enough to make me make up an excuse about how "fighting you isn't worth it," which is code for "having my face smashed in isn't worth it because I really like my face."

But for some reason, I stood my ground that day. Maybe it was because Miguel had been hanging out with us so much that he seemed like one of the boys. We were sitting in his living room, taking bong rips and attempting to cash entire bowls of Mexican schwag weed in one hit. Miguel finished his bowl. Donny finished his. I sucked hard and took as much as I could before coughing halfway through. Everyone laughed at me, which was nothing new, but then Miguel began chanting, "Faggot Ass Lungs! Woo!" He said this over and over for the better part of an hour, until I'd had enough.

"Faggot Ass Lungs! Woo!"

"Dude, shut the fuck up. I'm not used to finishing whole bowls of food like you. You don't just finish bowls of weed; you also appear to have polished off a few bowls of carnitas."

Miguel, who wasn't used to any of us talking back to him, looked perplexed and irritated. "Fool, I'll slap the shit out of you."

"I don't give a fuck," I yelled. Go ahead and do it!"

What was I saying? I did give a fuck. I didn't give a fuck.

"Wussup then, you little white bitch, let's step outside."

Miguel stood up and began walking outside, ready to fuck me up.

Jamie, DJ, and Joey all looked at me as if I was insane. But I got up. Fuck it.

Once outside, I took a brick from Miguel's neighbor's front yard, presumably to crack Miguel in the face with. I'm not sure how I intended to leap up and do that, but it didn't matter.

"Why don't you drop that fuckin brick and fight me man-to-man, you little white faggot-ass-lunged bitch?" Miguel said."

When I stood next to Miguel, I looked more like a kid he was babysitting than a man, but I dropped the brick and rushed him, screaming.

"Fuck you!""

We clashed. Actually, I crashed into Miguel's stomach. It was like the Ghostbusters going after the forty-foot Stay Puft Marshmallow Man or Westey fighting Andre the Giant in The Princess Bride. I ran into his stomach and nothing happened.

Without movement, there is no effect.

"Fuck," I thought. "What have I gotten myself into?""

I looked over at Joey and Donny, but their eyes held no answers for me.

"You fucked up now, you little bitch," Miguel said into my ear.

"Believe me, I know," I said.

Miguel, perhaps bemused by my bravery, never punched me. He simply laid his weight on me, collapsing me to the ground. I was trapped, helpless under the weight of his blubbery expression. He began to laugh. He was always laughing.

"Are you done, faggot lung?""

"I guess," I wheezed, my lungs popping like a novelty squeeze toy's head.

"Just say, I've got faggot lungs, woo!" And I'll let you up."

"Are you serious?" I began to merge with the gravel beneath me, sinking into the earth."

"Hell yeah, bitch, serious as a heart attack, woo!""

Oh God. "Fine. "I've got faggot lungs," I conceded.

"Say woo."

I was losing consciousness. "What?"

"Woo, motherfucker, say woo," Miguel grinned like a Mexican Cheshire cat.

"Wooooooooooooooooooo," I exclaimed.

Miguel rolled off of me, and I felt a relief greater than a thousand orgasms.

As I lay there, waiting for my body to re-inflate like Wile E. Coyote after being flattened by a steamroller, I felt a strong sense of accomplishment, as if I'd fought a grizzly bear. Sure, I'd lost, but at least I'd tried.

Miguel sat next to me for a few minutes, smoking a cigarette. He stroked my shoulder.

"You were pretty low back there, man. rale!"

I smirked. "Órale."

"If you ever want to join the Nortenos, let me know." We're currently launching a new white boy expansion program."

"Thank you, Miguel, but I'm more down with the Surenos," Miguel said angrily. I urinated on myself and whimpered, "I'm kidding." Miguel stared at me for a second, death in his eyes, and then burst out laughing. He grabbed my shoulder and drew me closer to him. "Órale! You're hilarious!"

Larry and my mother had left town the previous weekend, presumably to get away from me. I was supposed to stay at Donny's, but with an empty house and no parents, what was I supposed to do?

I broke into my own house and invited everyone over. It's time to party. Joey Zalante brought mushrooms. We all sat around and broke the mushrooms into pieces, which we then downed with handfuls of CornNuts to mask the taste. Classy. There is no better way to start a psychedelic trip than with chile-picante-flavored CornNuts. That's how the ancient Mayans did it.

After the mushrooms, we snorted Donny's Ritalin. Speed and mushrooms—to make the cartoons play faster.

We were high, so stealing the car seemed like a great idea. Larry and my mother had spent years slapping together a VW bug out of two non-working cars. It was a colossal eyesore. My mother and Larry had been foolish enough to leave it at home, multicolored, unpainted, and rusted through the floorboards, believing I'd be too embarrassed to be seen in it. They had no idea that the mushrooms I'd be eating would transform me into a Transformer. Transformers were a favorite of mine.

We all piled into the bug, and Joey took the wheel. I didn't know how to drive. None of us had a driver's license. We grabbed some forties and a bag of weed before heading into Tilden Park, a sort of wilderness reserve in Oakland's hills.

We drove through the hills, pounding our beers and looking for a spot to smoke and gaze out at the city. We went too far at one point and attempted to turn around by pulling onto a steep dirt hill on the side of the road and rolling back down it in the opposite direction. At least, that was the plan. What happened was that the bug began to tip over backward, ready to flip on its end, due to the instability of the dirt, the shoddiness of the car, and the weight of five idiotic stoners in the backseat. We all jumped out, like an insane Chinese fire drill, and coaxed the car back onto the ground by hand. We sat in the car, panting in fear, and decided to stop driving and smoke right there on the side of the road.

Then, as if on cue, light flooded the car at the exact moment we lit the pipe. The cops. We got caught.

Fuck.

This was it. My mother told me that if I was arrested again, I'd be sent to a group home or, worse, to study Talmud in Sea Gate with my father. Armed with that information, I promptly stole her car. These were the kinds of decisions I made.

I couldn't believe how stupid I was. I always seemed to choose the dumbest thing to do in the face of the most obvious answer in the world. It was as if I couldn't control my own mind. It was pointless to try to figure that out now. There were more pressing matters at hand.

I threw the pipe out the passenger window and sat staring straight ahead, trying to force the pot smell out of the car.

The cop walked from his car, right over to the pipe, and handed it back to me with a grin, saying, "I think you dropped this." I pretended I'd never seen a pipe before.

"What is this thing?"

"You mean the pipe I just saw you drop out the window that's still warm from you smoking from it?" Is that what you're asking?"

I sighed. I was fucked.

"So," the cop began, "what are you guys doing?"

I took a deep breath. "All right, here's the thing. I just finished the finishing touches on this car—as you can see, it's a bit of a project car!" I laughed hysterically as my speedy shroomy brain spun into action, pulling the next line of nonsense directly from the sky.

"Then I thought, well, jeez, just like a boat needs a maiden voyage, so does a car!" AM I RIGHT? So we piled in and took her for a spin; in fact, we were just on our way home when you stopped us, which I appreciate because it's like... TIME TO GO HOME! Is this correct?"

The speed was coursing through my veins, pumping me up. However, Miguel, seated in the backseat, leaned forward and broke the awkward silence.

"He's lying to you, Officer!"

What. The. Fuck.

Every head in the car turned in surprise as Miguel approached.

"He just stole his parents' shit!"

Miguel had experienced a psychic breakdown. Or so it appeared. Even the cop was taken aback by what a strange snitch Miguel was.

I looked at the cop. I exhaled deeply.

"Look," I began, defeated, "this is my parents' car." I lied to you because I'm completely screwed if I get caught again. Sorry for the swearing; my mother allows it. She is deaf. Like, totally..."

I was cuing up the string section, hoping for pity. If lying isn't an option, perhaps a heavy dose of the truth will.

"It's difficult having deaf parents, and I sometimes act out to get attention." They just told me that if I screw up again, I'll be sent to a group home or something. I know I screwed up, and if you could just give me a chance and let me call my sister and have her come meet me and drive the car home, you'd be essentially saving my life. This is it. I could be sent away, fall through the cracks in the system, contract AIDS, and die. You could also let me call my sister."

For a split second, the cop looked at me, his face a mix of pity and amusement.

He smiled. "All right. Let's call your sister."

I tried not to look surprised. Amazing. He was going to let us go. All I had to do was call my sister. There is only one problem. My only sister was ten years old and lived in Brooklyn.

"You follow me down the hill and we can call your sister from a pay phone when we get back into town."

To be more specific, a real-life police officer allowed a drunk, high, unlicensed kid in a stolen car to drive down a windy mountain road at night. Sometimes there is only one set of footprints in the sand. That's when God takes you. And that night, he carried me with a gentleness that said, "I forgive you for the phone sex, I totally get it."

Donny turned to face me and exhaled, the first of us to do so in a long time. "How is this happening?"" He inquired.

We arrived at the bottom of the hill panting, our hearts pounding in fear, certain that this was all a trick.

I sighed as we approached the bottom of the hill. "Here goes nothing." "Hey, Miguel, thanks for your assistance back there."

Miguel, on the other hand, was too preoccupied with his own thoughts to hear me.

I opened the car door and walked to the phone like a convicted murderer on his way to the gallows. I locked my gaze on the pay phone, willing my mind to work quickly. I picked up the phone and dialed a neighbor named Seena. We'd hardly ever talked on the phone. Hopefully she won't be too surprised to learn she's my sister.

I inserted a quarter into the phone like a slot machine gambler. "God," I prayed, taking refuge in the coward's prayer, "I know two times in one night is a lot to ask, but... help me out here?""

The phone rang...

A click. A sleepy voice. An angel.

"Hello?"

"Sis! My sister! Oh, the girl with whom I share parents! It's me, your brother!"

Seena, perplexed and irritated, spit back, "Huh? Brother? Why are you calling me this late? Wait, why are you calling me at all?"

"Totally!" I said, masking my relief as brotherly love. "Look, I stole Mom's car." I know I'm a moron! Anyway, the cops are here, and they said they'd let me go if you just come pick up the car and drive it home."

A pause. I could hear the gears turning in Seena's head.

"Oh, no. Is there a cop nearby? Are you pretending to be my brother to avoid trouble?"

DING.

I turned to face the cop. I gave a big smile.

"Yes!" I yelled, hoping.

"You fucking asshole. If I come out there, you'd better get me high."

"Of course!" Hearing her agree to rescue me was so incredible that I could have ejaculated a river of relief all over the sidewalk and paddled home in it." My sister was coming! My sweet, sweet, phony sister.

"I adore you, sis!" I panted.

"Go fuck yourself," she snarled. You know how my sister can be!

"She's on her way!" I said to the cop."I could hear my friends cheering like we'd won the lottery from inside the bug." This was a good night.

Seena arrived bleary-eyed and glaring at me, just like a real sister would. In that moment, I loved her more than I had ever loved anyone.

"I'm so sorry about my brother, Officer," she said as she pulled up. "I was sleeping and didn't hear the boys take the car out."

The boys. She should have won an Oscar.

"No problem at all, glad you could help," the officer said with a smile.

"My boyfriend will drive my car home, and I'll take the bug." Once again, thank you."

With a grin, the officer looked at Seena's blond hair and anti-Semitic features.

"No problem. "You know, you two look exactly alike." He smiled. Was that sarcasm? Who was this cop?

Just then, Dean Stockwell appeared, and the cop quantum-leaped away (nerd joke!).

Or, rather, we all drove away, waving goodbye to the most amazing cop since Robocop. We drove home in silence, awestruck by the miracle we had witnessed. All except Miguel, who awoke from his mushroom coma, leaned forward, and asked, "Hey, what just happened?"

I might have hit him if he hadn't been so big and Mexican. As it was, I just laughed. When we arrived at my house, Seena turned to me and said, "There's no way you're going to get popped twice in one night, so let's take this hooptie out and have some fun."

It made sense to me. I dashed upstairs, grabbed more booze, and we carried on with our evening, the majesties of the Lord forgotten the moment a suggestion for more fun was made. Have you ever pushed a Bug on its last legs into the 100-mile-per-hour zone? It will cause you to recall previous lives. Seena drove the Bug down Highway 580, laughing at our good fortune. The poor little engine screamed as we sped down the straightaway, attempting to keep up with our party. As the needle redlined, the car's radio, which hadn't worked in decades, squealed to life, blaring oldies into our insane night. My mind was racing as we drove back to my house at four a.m. I was shaking with speed and mushrooms, slurring with booze and pot; I was fucked. It seemed like a logical next step for me to snort some Zoloft at the time. Keep in mind that Zoloft has no psychoactive properties. But I figured, what the fuck, why not give it a shot? I shook a couple of pills in the kitchen by myself. I could hear my friends laughing and partying in the next room, but this rare delicacy I would keep to myself. I squinted at the pills, willing myself not to hear the thought that was creeping up the side of my head: "This is a really lousy idea." Instead, I chose to heed the other, much less logical but much more compelling thought, "What the hell, why not?" See what happens; it could be amazing. "Fuck it," is the great battle cry of the drug addict. It's the rebel yell we all yell as we charge into the stupid, ridiculous, dangerous pool of nonsense that we will inevitably drown in. My hands were trembling as I crushed the pills that had been messing with my brain chemistry for the past year. Chunks of the protective easy-swallow coating protruded from the white lines like coral rocks jutting out of a foamy surf, warning, "Bad idea! There will be pain ahead!" I grabbed my surfboard and dove in. I leaned down and snorted half a comically large line of Zoloft. The grit flew into my nose like sinking into quicksand in reverse. The back of my sinus cavity filled up in a split second, and the inside of my face caught fire. Pain shot through my head like the devil was giving me an ice-pick lobotomy. My head shot straight up as I slapped at my face, desperate to get it to go away. I ran screaming to the bathroom, hoping to find something to relieve the pain. I dashed to the sink and looked in the mirror. Scary. My right eye was literally bloodred. The right side of my face felt like a thousand little elves were aerating a lawn with spiky little golf shoes. I felt like I was going to die. There was poisonous pain shooting into my brain. Oddly, the left side of my face was just fine and looked like my handsome old self. I should have gone and fought Batman with a face like that (nerd joke!). Getting to that threshold of acceptance that you must come to in moments of great pain, I accepted that, perhaps, I was going to have a stroke. I waited. My face still hurt, so that meant it wasn't paralyzed. Tears were streaming down my face that were opaque with medicine. I think my eye turned purple. I crawled to my bedroom window and spent the next hour sitting there, spitting out loogies filled with rocks of Zoloft onto the sidewalk below. If a depressed dog had walked along just then, he could have lapped it up and tasted happiness for the first time in dog years. I slunk out of my perch, my poison face having backed off to enough of an extent that I could walk upright. I walked into my living room, where my friends were all sitting and drinking with each other.

As I walked into the living room, everyone screamed.

"A zombie!" Jamie yelled. "This happened to my uncle!"

Seena wept.

Miguel crossed himself. "Dios Mío. Es El Diablo!"

Donny and Joey approached me like I was a feral animal.

"Dude," Donny whispered. "You all right?"

Right! My eye.

"Oh, this? Ahh, this is nothing. I was just snorting a little Zoloft, you know? Seein' what would happen."

"Looks like you've been snorting a little cyanide, bro." Joey sounded genuinely concerned.

"I'm fine, I'm fine. I can see the future in my right eye, but other than that, I'm fine." I laughed and coughed up a full pill of Zoloft. "Anyway, let's go up to the roof."

One by one, we all, even Miguel's huge ass, climbed up to my roof. The bastard sun was making its threats on the night, revealing to us all that this dark night was going to crash to an end. Teenage vampires we were, sucking down whatever blood we could find in the bottom of a bottle. Donny and I stood there, looking over the city lights to the west, the purple-red middle finger of the sun to the east, passing a cigarette back and forth. Just me and my friend Donny smoking again. I felt okay. In charge. Alive. The magic luck of the drug addict had been sprinkled on me, and I'd had a night to remember. But drug-addict luck always runs out. I woke up the next day groggy, hungover, and ready to die. Donny was up and said something about going to the store to get booze. I threw him the keys and rolled over back to sleep. I woke up a few hours later to my grandmother's voice shrieking, "Wake up! Get up! Where is the car?"

Shit. The car. Where was the car?

Right! Donny. Fuck. I was pretty fucked. I'd been given a thousand second chances the night before, but I'd fucked up and lost anyway. But right then all I could do was vomit in my lap. I did so.

"Ugh, disgusting," my grandmother sneered. "Just like your grandfather." This was her version of the worst thing she could say to me. "Where is the car?"

"Well, I don't know in the classic sense of knowing. Well…"

I thought fast in what seemed like a pretty good lie in the moment.

"I…"

I remembered the radio from last night.

"I fixed the radio!"

"What?" my grandmother asked, confused.

"Yeah!" I yelled, gaining confidence. "I fixed the radio. I have a buddy who does that kind of repair work, and so I wheeled the bug down to his shop and fixed the radio to surprise Mom and Larry when they get back. Yep. That's where the car is now. The radio-fixing shop."

A pretty good, pretty high-grade lie. Jamie would have been proud.

"You pushed the car?" My grandmother looked dubious.

"Well, yeah! I didn't drive. I don't have a license. That's illegal! Duh."

"You pushed the car down the street to repair the radio?"

"Yes. Exactly." Why didn't she believe me? I was lying, but there was no way for her to know that.

"To repair the radio for your deaf mother."

I paused.

"You know, I totally didn't think of that! Ha ha!"

My grandmother looked less amused. Just then I heard the car pull back into the driveway. Saved!

"Well, there's the mechanic now, delivering the car!"

We walked downstairs together, me covered in vomit, my grandmother covered in doubt. Joey crawled out of the driver's seat with a bottle of Jack Daniel's in his hands.

"Hey, thanks for fixing the radio, champ!"

"Yeah." Joey stared at me, confused. "Anytime… champ."

I sat down in the driver's seat and looked up at my grandmother with a confident smile. "Here we go."

I smiled, flipped on the radio. Silence. Somehow the radio had rebroken itself. I felt God's hands snatch away from me. I crashed hard onto the sand. Apparently God, much like everyone else, was tired of my shit. Once again, I was fucked.

# CHAPTER 8

# "ILLEGAL BUSINESS"

I learned how to hustle money on a daily basis. Being a fifteen-year-old drug addict means always scraping and stealing money in order to get high. Nobody's paycheck is large enough to meet the cost of addiction. I had no employment, no possessions, just my wits and a psychopathic streak. My house has turned into a conundrum. How to get into locations where I didn't belong and then take stuff I didn't possess. I looked at locks for hours, trying to see how I could break them from different angles. A kitchen knife was transformed into a screwdriver. A doorstop was turned into a wedge to force open a door. I forced my house to give up its freedom. As the police beat on my front door, looking for a cat burglar who resembled the kid who lived inside, I scaled the walls on the outside of my own house and raced out the backdoor with a handful of cash. I gradually began collecting items from around the house and selling them for narcotics. I'd purge the house of items I didn't think would be missed. A little something here and there. I'd pull large atlases off the shelves and good hardcover volumes like The Power of Myth and A Guide to Western Civilization and sell them at the bookstore. I'd take stacks of CDs from Larry's collection and sell them at Amoeba Records. What a responsible company that was. They didn't even raise an eyebrow when they spotted a fifteen-year-old blurry-eyed youngster with sagging leggings and a Fila cap cocked to the side selling a handful of Wagner and Vivaldi CDs. I think they assumed I was more interested in Vivaldi's later work. They removed the stuff and gave me money without asking any questions. I took that money to the dope house, and they gave me the real deal. My parents were the only ones that lost out. I accepted cash and credit cards, CDs and books, and sold my own items as well as my grandmother's collections. Her jewels had vanished. When I needed smokes, I stole my mother's food stamps and walked to Safeway, where I purchased three packs and delivered them to the back of the store, where the coffee grinder was. I'd stuff the packs into a one-pound coffee bag and fill it with arabica beans to disguise my loot. I'd then confidently proceed to the front of the store and drop the beans.

"Just the coffee then?" the clerk would inquire, mistrust in her eyes.

"Yep! That's all!" I'd cheerfully respond.

"Coffee with cinnamon hazelnuts and nothing else?" "At 1:00 a.m." She sensed something was awry but couldn't pinpoint what it was.

"What can I say… I'm a hazel-NUT!" I gave a wide grin.

I'd give up the food handouts and pretend to be a victim of bad luck. When I wanted alcohol, I went straight to the hard liquor section and grabbed a bottle. It would be in my pants before I had a chance to pause and before anyone noticed me. I stole hundreds of liquor bottles. I usually drank Seagram's Extra Dry Gin, which had a rough bottle that held my waistline and kept the bottle from slipping out. I'd also get a Maker's Mark bourbon, which came with a hand-melted wax topper that I could pull out and lay on my belt for traction, preventing it from sliding down my pant leg and crashing onto the floor, disclosing my crime and wasting my medicine. I got really good at it. It evolved into an art form. I'd be in and out of the grocery shop in under five minutes. Nobody expected me to appear. I'd glide up to the front counter and ask an inane question that would give me an excuse to go right out again as soon as the bottle's coldness touched my waist.

"Excuse me?" Pudgy and innocent, I inquired. "Do you guys have birdcages?"

Now I knew that no Safeway in Oakland, or in history, had ever sold a birdcage. But they had no idea I was aware of this.

"No, sweetie, we don't carry those." The hapless clerk attempted to lessen the blow.

"Aw, guy! I had just found an injured pigeon and was looking for a home for it. So, best wishes!"

"Good luck, sweetie." She'd follow me like a boy hero as I limped away, terrified that the bottle would fall out.

"And he's got a limp, too," she'd probably think. "That poor, sweet crippled child."

"God bless us!" I'd turn around and yell. "God bless us every one!"

My buddies were impressed by my thievery, but they also used it to their advantage. They knew I was anxious for their acceptance, so they took advantage of it to acquire free alcohol.

"C'mon, man, get us some drink!" Joey would scream at me. "I'd do it myself, but you're just so good at it!"

"Aw, I'm all right," I'd murmur, my face flushed with pride.

My mother tried to rein me in again after I was arrested, with the car gone and evidence of my lost weekend scattered about the home, and my grandma yelling about my shoplifting exploits. Of course, the problem with my mother preventing me from entering her room to prevent me from stealing was that she was a very forgetful lady. Sure, she'd lock the doors and windows, but she'd also leave her purse laying about, its gaping mouth wide open, as if encouraging me to take a little, just enough to feel okay. My mother was broke, and I knew it was bad on some level, but I couldn't help myself. I took full advantage of her forgetfulness, knowing she'd never recall how much money she had in her handbag on any given day. Stealing from your deaf, welfare-aided mother is the same as murdering a man. In any case, I imagine it is. You feel sick the first time you do it and wonder what happened to you. Then, in an instant, it transforms from a horrible secret to exactly what you need to do. It is simply a source of revenue. You then proceed to steal from your granny. I stole massively. I stole heinously. I stole like a beast. Oh, no, animals do not steal. I stole like a jerk. Yeah, like a jerk. I felt like a bad person at times, but I usually just did what I had to do. I'd push aside my feelings about what I was doing and replace them with the satisfaction that comes from knowing your period of agony is coming to an end. I could feel my life falling into quicksand, but I couldn't see why with clear eyes. I was persuaded that every time I was ready to be dragged out of the hole, an adult would appear and force me back down. I was surrounded by groups of people who claimed to have been tasked with assisting me, but all they appeared to do was send me to locations that made me feel even more shattered and damaged than the last. They just ever locked my windows and my life. They only served to remind me of what a messed-up piece of garbage I was. My pals, as bad as they were, never said I was worse than them. Only that we were all bad at the same time. That's why we stayed close. We were as thick as thieves. We were thieves, after all.

# CHAPTER 9

# "IT'S ALL BAD"

Donny returned to Oakland just in time for me to hit rock bottom. We were fifteen years old. He and his father had been drinking together, and he'd been slipping off to snort drugs in the bathroom, and it came as no surprise that their living situation hadn't worked out. Donny returned to town battered and depressed. I went to the airport with Donny's mother to pick him up. New Mexico had made him a new Mexican. During his time in New Mexico, he became involved with a Mexican street gang. I can't recall which one it was because they have so many. His socks were pulled up like cholo's, and his silky curls were shaved bald to give the appearance of a prison inmate. Donny's mother turned to the backseat as soon as she parked to explain the rules to him. We were half-way out the car door.

"Where the hell are you two going?" she yelled, terrified that things were about to revert to their pre-Donny state.

"Out! "Please give me a night to myself!" Donny shouted at his mother, and we were off into the night again. I'm heading to Oakland.

This was our town. It's all set for us to take over. But we both realized we were drifting apart. Screw it. Ignore reality and revel in the damp. We crept inside an abandoned house on College Avenue and crept to the top, to a small balcony with a view of the city. I took out the ingredients for a blunt I'd brought just for the occasion. With my fingernail, I split a Phillies Blunt cigar down the center, cheap brown tobacco oozing out like sofa stuffing. I split the cigar's leafy shell in half and wrenched it open with my two fingers while sprinkling bright green bud in place of the garbage that had previously been there. I stuffed it full of goodies, aiming to give my old pal a regal welcome. I ran my tongue down the serrated opening to seal the two sides of the cigar wrapper together and dried it with my lighter. We smoked when we had achieved perfection. I coughed, he coughed, and we smoked the night away. We climbed to the roof and flung building supplies at cars while the world swam behind us and the blunt was cashed. It occurred to me that I'd done something similar with another best friend only a few years before. It seems like a lifetime ago. It felt like I was living in the life of someone else. I merely had a hazy idea that was my life. I didn't recognize Richard Lilly any longer, but more importantly, I didn't recognize the overweight kid who stood next to him throwing oranges. I had nothing in common with him. I was a completely different person. My appetite had been hindered by years of psychiatric medication and psychedelic drug use, so I was taller and leaner. My vision was hazy. My hair was slicked back with a thick layer of Tres Flores hair grease, which poured down onto my face and encircled it with an acne-ringed chinstrap beard. As usual, I sagged my jeans six inches below my waist. I strolled like a pimp. I appeared to be a fool. A hazardous idiot.

We descended, and Donny said, "There's supposed to be a party tonight, so let's roll."

I dashed into Lucky's, and Donny trailed behind me about thirty seconds later. The moment we came into the store, all eyes were on us. We now appeared to be criminals. There was no childlike innocence to shield us from inquisitive eyes. More drastic measures were required. Donny turned around by the bakery and emerged in front of the business. "I don't feel well!" he yelled. He then collapsed, foaming and shaking, in the grand mal performance of a lifetime. The employees dropped what they were doing and dashed over to assist the unfortunate epileptic gangbanger in front of them. They didn't spot the blur of a slightly obese young Jew carrying a twenty-four pack of Budweiser running out the front door, barely steps away from the hubbub. Donny straightened up and rushed to his feet the moment he saw me sneak out the door.

"I think I'm starting to feel better now." Thank you very much!" We were gone in an instant after Donny waved goodbye. Another complication.

We reconvened at the BART station, jumped the turnstiles together, and dashed out to the suburbs. We were both sloppy drunk by the time we got to Pleasant Hill, and as we tromped down the escalator, we saw two enormous BART cops seated directly at our only exit. We simply resolved to return to Oakland by tagging up the train cars. It seemed like old times. I sat on the bench at the station, waiting for the train, and looked over at Donny.

I let out a sigh.

"This isn't working anymore," I said as opening open a Budweiser.

When Donny looked up at me, I knew he understood exactly what I meant.

I let out a sigh. "Like, is it normal? What are we doing? We're going nowhere and doing nothing. I keep expecting this thing to magically transform on its own. I keep waiting for the balance to move in my favor, but I'm beginning to believe it won't. I'm beginning to believe it will never change. Is this really my life?"

I looked at my pal, my old friend, expecting a laugh.

It did not arrive.

"I feel you." Donny peered over the ledge. Weary. Cracked. Dusted. "New Mexico screwed me over, man. It's insane over there. I'm completely messed up. "I, too, am at a loss for what to do."

"So now what?"

We were both confused.

DJ and Corey were on their way. Their time in jail had messed them up and scared them half-straight. Jamie had not been seen or heard from for several months. We assumed he was in jail, but there was no way of knowing.

Everyone had dispersed into the wind. Joey was high on coke and barely recognizable as a human being.

"The rehab I went to was a good place." "Perhaps we could go check in there," Donny mumbled, his voice trembling.

"Check ourselves into rehab?" I couldn't believe it.

"I'm not sure, man. I'm not sure. Nothing will change if nothing changes. "Do you understand what I mean?" Donny appeared deflated.

"I get what you mean. However, I do not require rehabilitation. That nonsense has never worked for anyone. I'm going to take a break for a time. I need to get my act together. I'll quit now. We should come to a halt."

Donny was skeptical. "I'm down, I guess."

I finished my Bud and gazed out the window at the BART tracks. What was I going to do to change?

The next day, I came into my mother's room and triumphantly declared that I was going to get my sh*t together. She'd heard hollow promises before. The king of hollow promises, the drug addict. My mother gave me a tired expression. She appeared to be elderly. Tired. I'm sick of hoping for me. Tired of attempting and failing. To be truthful, I was also fed up with failing. I honestly believed that things would improve on their own. I couldn't believe I was going to fail. I saw my brother's golden brick road to success as something that should have been mine but was just out of grasp. I couldn't figure out how he'd encountered the same crap as me and always managed to turn it into gold. He was a Jewish Rumpelstiltskin, spinning dung into degrees. I always believed things would simply flip. That, without my intervention, the tipping point would be reached and my life would be restored. My slimy world would return to normalcy. I anticipated that any day now, I'd receive a phone call that would transform everything...

RIIIIING!

"Hello?"

"Hello, is this Mr. Kasher?"

"This is he."

"Hi, Mr. Kasher, this is College calling."

"College?"

"Yes, Mr. Kasher, College... College!" We've been following your development for a time now, and while we're aware you've been experiencing some challenges recently, we believe it's clear you're far too intelligent to fail. Perhaps even a genius."

"That's what I've been saying!!!"

"Exactly! So, in any case, we're willing to overlook the repeated ninth-grade flunking..."

"It's more complicated than it appears. I've suffered several major setbacks, none of which were my fault!"

"Our research proves it!" We are willing to overlook all of those obstacles and offer you to join us, tuition free, housing and board provided... here... at COLLEGE!"

That call was never going to arrive, I realized. This was not going to change unless I did. Nothing will change if nothing changes.

"I've decided to get my shit together," I said to my mom, triumphantly stepping into her room, ready to accept her thanks. She was unimpressed. Okay, I'd said it before, but this time I meant it. My mother looked up at me, her eyes filled with doubt. "I wish I could believe that."

"Well, you can." I was offended by her implication.

"I'm beginning to believe you'll never change. I wish I had the guts to kick you out. That's what Dr. Susan suggests I do. I'm too frail. That is true love. "Love weakens you." My mother's fingers flew in the light, trails pouring from them, playing tricks on my drug-addled brain as she signed this for me.

"I'm saying I want to change right now." "I'm declaring that I'm going to change."

My mother sighed. "So change then."

So I'd also lost her.

Whatever, I'd show her, and everyone else who felt I was doomed to fail. I was going to show them who the fuck I was. I went over to Monk's house. He'd gone from being a terrific friend to just being my drug dealer. Old recollections only gave me a 24-hour credit grace period. When I knocked on his door, he slid the privacy screen to the side, revealing my identity. He looked exactly like a real drug dealer.

"Hey, man," I said as I handed him $20 for yesterday's bag and a new one for today, money I'd snatched from my mother's handbag while she was telling me I'd never change. One more twenty. The final one.

"This is it," I said to Monk.

"What is it?" he inquired, clearly uninterested.

I gave him a serious look. "I'm out of the game, man, I'm out." I need to get my act together. This is my final bag. "I'm finished."

Monk raised his head. As he handed me the package, he appeared nearly impressed. "That's cool, man, whatever you need."

When I returned to his house the next day to buy a bag, he came to the door, looked at me, and sneered in hatred.

I smiled and extended my cash. "Hey, lemme hold something, man."

Monk glanced at me as if he couldn't believe what I was saying. He shook his head and extended a bag to me.

"What the hell are you doing here?" he demanded. "You said you were out of the game yesterday, and here you are today." You definitely have a problem, dude."

I'm here to inform you that if your drug dealer ever performs an intervention on you, it's time to seek treatment. That's when I decided to resign. Every night, I'd give up. Every night, I vowed to myself that I would never do it again. I had to come to a halt. I have to stop causing others pain. I needed to get my act together. I had to finish high school before I turned thirty. I had to refrain from peeing somewhere else than the toilet. Every night, I gave up. Every morning, I awoke forgetting the vows I'd made to myself the night before. I'd feel the urge to go high and be at my dealer's house or Safeway with a bottle of gin in my pants before I had a chance to dispute with myself. It wasn't at all what you'd expect. I didn't give up. I had forgotten. I didn't engage in a wrestling bout with my conscience, battling it back and forth until I gave up. Rather, it appeared that I lacked a conscience. It wasn't a battle between good and evil.

# CHAPTER 10

# "WHO AM I?"

This was unexpected. For years, I'd been telling myself what every addict recognizes as a familiar refrain: "I could quit if I wanted to, I just don't want to." Then came the day I wished for. Then it dawned on me that I couldn't. The moment you realize you've lost control is when you know you need it.

Donny was having similar outcomes.

We'd get together and talk about our plans to sober up while sipping forties of St. Ides.

"Perhaps we should go back to that rehab," I suggested, afraid.

"You can't stop either?" Donny burst out laughing.

"Naw." I looked down at my hands, which were wrapped around that heavy bottle, beer sweat trickling down my fingers. I finished that forty and made my decision.

When I told my mother about my plan, she looked hopeful.

"I'm going to Kaiser and check in," I said.

"That's fantastic. That makes me very delighted."

For a change, Donny and I went to the Kaiser Outpatient Adolescent Chemical Dependency Program in Walnut Creek and told them the truth. We were admitted right away. I realized the moment I arrived that I despised them just as much as I hated the people before them, just as I loathed every fucking adult with control over me. Oakland Public Schools had also noted that I had dropped out again. It didn't really matter. I was a bother to them. I was causing more trouble than I was worth. My mother made a fuss and got me on the waiting list for Spraings Academy, which she was confident would be the answer for me. Oakland agreed to finance my therapy for another year. I'd go to another fucking counselor. Oh delight.

When I stepped into Kaiser's group that first day, I understood I'd made a tremendous fucking mistake. The kids seemed okay at first, but then the group started. "Hey, everyone," said a voice from the back of the room as the door opened. It's great to see everyone."

That voice seemed familiar to me. I'd heard about it somewhere. I turned to look. Tim the Fucking Hammock. Kaiser program's new lead counselor. My adversary from New Bridge. The guy who loathed me and baited me at my previous rehab was suddenly the newly minted head counselor at my latest one, neatly transferred to Kaiser just in time to sabotage my attempt to get my sh*t together. I could never seem to get a break. He gave me a wink. He gave a wide smile. That fucking scumbag, I thought. This was going to be a disaster. Nonetheless, I was eager to give it a shot. Every night, I tried. Every morning, I fail. That hunger couldn't be satisfied by rehab. I was becoming increasingly concerned. I sat in the group, wondering what was the point of it all. Every day, Tim entered into group and scoffed at me. He sat down with us and lectured us on how to change. Nobody paid attention. Donny and I spent hours fucking around in groups, teasing Tim for the wart on his cheek that had grown in the years since I'd seen him at New Bridge. Donny and I would take turns circling the room, making eye contact with the other youngsters in the group and fucking with them. We'd convince them that they had something on their face and chuckle as they rubbed away fictitious stains.

When the group psychiatrist, Dr. Dale Dallas, came in to observe Tim's leadership skills, Donny and I would yell at him, "Wokka Wokka Wokka!"

What? He had the exact same appearance as Fozzie Bear. We'd rage over wrongs Tim had never done.

"Dr. Dallas, is it normal for Tim to be holding my penis while I give a urine sample?" I laughed.

"That's not a funny accusation at all." Dr. Dallas squirmed uneasily.

"Okay, fine, Tim never held my dick, but can you tell us one more time what life was like with Kermit and Miss Piggy?" As Donny cackled one last "Wokka Wokka Wokka!!" I'd inquire.

We passed away laughing. Tim's face flushed bright red. Dale Dallas promptly exited the room. I was attempting. I was, but I didn't know how to try. Like New Bridge, Kaiser chanted, "Get rid of your friends, you'll never get better surrounded by those guys."

How could I possibly accomplish that? No way. I'd just be tough. Every night after group, Donny and I would return to Oakland and catch up with DJ, Corey, and anyone else was around.

"I'm not drinking tonight, guys!" I'd tell them over and over. I said it firmly, encouraging Donny to agree. It never arrived.

"More for us!" DJ would slur and swig from the bottle.

We sat in a circle, passing the bottle from person to person. The closer it got to me, the less vividly I could grasp my resolution not to drink. It was on its way to me next.

Oh, forget about that. Oblivion and a drink. The discomfort didn't go away, but it did subside. When I look into a bottle of gin, my memory becomes foggy.

I staggered home, burning drunk, stinking of gin, and on the verge of passing out.

I stumbled into the home and hobbled my way to the restroom.

My mother stood vigil at the top of the steps, waiting. "Is this what it looks like when you get sober?" she angry, her hopes dashed yet again. "You're drunk."

"A bit!" I laughed and shoved her aside, making my way to the restroom for a great drunken shit.

She screamed after me, but I ignored her and slammed the door in her face. I sat down on the toilet and started defecating inebriated. That's when my mother slammed the bathroom door open like an enraged cop.

"I'm sick and tired of you pushing me around!" she said as she charged me like a linebacker.

"Mom, I'm shitting!" was the only logical response.

She didn't even slow down. She charged straight at me, yelling angrily, "FUCK YOU!!!!!"

In dread, my eyes widened. Contact. She lunged into me and wrestled me off the toilet, dragging me down onto the bathroom floor with a trail of poo still trailing behind her. I threw her off me, my pants around my ankles and shit everywhere, as her hands scratched and smacked at my face. I took her hand in mine and bit down hard. Her skin popped between my teeth, and her blood shot into my mouth. I smacked her across the face. I jolted her. She sobbed her way out of there. I'm on the bathroom floor, covered in shit and blood, tears, and rage. I felt like that baby racing down the birth canal. "What is he?" my mother inquired once more. I was completely unaware. Is it true that I'm no longer human? I'm a fucking beast. I'm a beast. The cops arrived. My mother dialed their number. Oh, fuck. I'm too inebriated for it. I dozed off, hoping that everything would go away. My mind was racing the next morning when I awoke. That rush of recollection of what I accomplished returned to me.

"Hey, Mom," I sobbed.

My mother turned to face me. Cold and irritated. Emotions are vanished. There was no disappointment. My mother's completed police report was sitting next her.

"They're sending us a date for you to appear in court." "They said it'd be a few months," my mother stated matter-of-factly.

"A court appearance? "What did you do, Ma?" This was unbelievable to me.

"There was nothing I did. The cops did. "They're sending us a date for you to go to trial," she said again, turning her back on me and turning on the television. I could tell the discussion was over. My mother had enrolled me in a juvenile first-offense court program, which was the most trouble she could get me into that night. She filed charges after becoming frustrated and felt that I needed to be taught a lesson, and I went to trial months later. It was a kangaroo court, where every single defendant was found guilty and sentenced to anger management classes and community service weekends while humiliated and wearing a bright neon safety vest. I approached the workstation with my head down, my vest dangling like a dunce cap, declaring me unsuitable for human consumption. It was a thousand-yard walk to work furlough check-in. My fellow juvenile delinquents evaluated me.

"Ay, man," one of the children said to another. "Whachu in here for?"

"Grand theft auto," a pimply black kid answered. "And how about you?"

"I robbed a liquor store."

Pimples gave me a sidelong glance. "What about you, white boy?"

"I bit my mama," I yipped. "Better watch out before I bite you, too."

After that, the kids pretty much abandoned me. I went about my work, minding my own business. Making new acquaintances was the last thing on my mind. Once again, I'd gotten myself into some stupid thing without my knowledge. But before that trial, I had to return to Kaiser and face the music of what I'd done in front of all my peers. Tim was waiting for me, ready with the information he required. He was well aware of what I'd been up to. He seemed ecstatic at the possibility of calling me out in front of everyone.

"Do you want to tell us about what happened last weekend?" he inquired, seeming to be concerned.

"Not really, Tim. No, not really." What was this jerk trying to do with me? Trying to reach out to me? Yeah, right.

"Well, after an incident like the one your mother told me about, we can't continue here without you discussing it." It's a big thing." Tim crossed his arms.

"I thought we weren't supposed to cross our arms, Tim." "Don't you realize that's a sign of defensiveness?"

"Making smart-ass comments isn't going to get you out of this," Tim stated emphatically.

"Please leave me alone." Just stop fucking pressuring me."

I was on the verge of crying. I was embarrassed and perplexed. But I wasn't about to tell him that. He's trying to get me to accept this nonsense in front of a bunch of kids? No way.

"Well, then, we might need to ask you to leave the group." Tim sighed and crossed his legs.

"You'd like that." Nobody cares that I'm finally attempting to quit. Nobody wants me to get better; they only want to speak about how messed up I am. So, kick me out. "I don't care anymore."

We sat in quiet for thirty seconds. A standoff.

"Let's take a break, guys." Tim looked around the group as if they were all in on something I wasn't. Only Donny was on my side, and he was high as fuck. I was certain of it. "Take five and we'll regroup for family session."

Session with the family. Ugh. My mother would be there, bandaged. Everybody's parents would be there, disgustedly glaring at me. I couldn't deal with it. Donny and I got onto the elevator, eager to go smoke and relax. I couldn't stop shaking. A hand darted in as the elevator doors closed. The door reopened as Nails flashed the sensor. Pantera Neck. We dubbed this lady Pantera Neck because of her shaved high back rocker haircut. She jumped into my elevator, giving me the stink eye.

"The fuck are you staring at me like that for?" I snarled at her.

"I don't like you. "You give Tim too much attitude," she frowned. Wasn't she just flirting with me last week?

"Lucky me, I don't give a fuck about your opinion of me." I told Donny to ignore this jerk.

"Fuck you, don't turn your back on me." She grabbed my shoulder and yanked me toward her.

I shoved her away from me, saying, "Hands to yourself, ho!"

She leaped at me, her hands twirling madly like a savage cat's. Her manicured nails raked a scarlet trail down my cheek. Did she just cut me?

A drop of blood dripped down my face like a tear, reminding me of the blood I let from my mother's hand. I snapped. You see, the powerlessness I suffered at the hands of all the women in my life, my mother, grandmother, and Dr. Susan, manifested itself in overcompensation in the rest of the world. I would strike out at the few girls in my life for any minor insult. I'd rant and humiliate them viciously, waiting for tears and a collapse. I had no notion at the time that I was wresting power from them that I had never had over the real ladies in my life, my mother and grandmother. Of course, I didn't consider the bigger picture—I just snapped. I jumped on Pantera Neck, snapping and shoving her up against the elevator wall, yelling, "Don't ever fuckin' put your hands on me, you tweaker bitch!" I shook her, grabbed a hold of her hair, and yanked her head back. She spit at me. Donny ran over to stop me just as the elevator reached the ground floor and the doors opened to see all of my colleagues staring at me with this chick in my hands, their mouths agape. They raced in and yanked me off her.

It's time for a family session!

Tim dragged into group ten minutes later, having just debriefed with Dr. Dallas in the corridor. The elephant in the living room was myself. I could feel the tension in the room. I'd felt it before. I'd lived my entire life as the "identified patient." I was used to being the topic of talk wherever I went. I used to be the issue. Every eye in that room was on me, silently accusing me of being the worst of the worst. Maybe I was.

"What? "I'm the one who got cut!" My face was streaming with blood. I wiped it away with my sleeve.

Pantera Neck and her entire family stared at me from across the room, death in their eyes.

"Sorry?" I shrugged.

I was humiliated. I'm sitting here looking like a hulk. How did I get here?

Worst of all, my mom's interpreter that night was this guy I'd always looked up to. Mike Hicks. A cool interpreter. It may not seem like much to you, but interpreters were a common occurrence in my life by that point. There were so many meetings involving me that I needed an interpreter. They sat at the back, like the unnoticed third party. A passive channel for the information that bore my sins. They were well-versed in all of my secrets. They were bound by a code of ethics that pledged them to confidentiality and nonjudgment, much like the Federation of Planets from Star Trek, but I knew better. I knew I was a bad fit for them. I was rude and cruel to interpreters. Nobody liked me. Except Mike. I knew he enjoyed interpreting for me. Mostly because he didn't resign like the previous interpreters who had come to the family session. Mike, like me, was the kid of two deaf parents. He wore leather ties and signed as if he understood what he was doing. He had long hair and a chimney sweep, E-Street mustache. He's a cool dude. He, an ex-drinker, didn't seem to be judging me like every other adult in my clinical lethargy. He reminded me of myself.

Everyone else's eyes were on me. Even Donny looked at me as if to say, "I can't help you."

Nobody could. Tim spoke up.

"After today's group, and especially after the incident in the elevator, I'm afraid we'll have to ask you to leave the program." I'm sorry." I almost believed Tim right then and there. He appeared to be dissatisfied. Was that possible? I sighed.

"I'm the one with the gash on my face." Why don't you get rid of her?"

Pantera Dad pounced at me, his eyes bulging from his skull. If it hadn't been for his wife, I might have been the first fatality in the Kaiser Adolescent Chemical Dependency Program.

IT'S BEEN ONE DAY SINCE OUR LAST WORKPLACE ACCIDENT (MURDER! ), according to a sign in the break room.

"OK, I understand. This time, I truly tried." I stood up and went to the door.

Tim raised his head to look at me. He didn't wink this time. He looked at my mother. "If you'd like, you can stay in family session without your boy and we can discuss a plan for his future."

My mother's name. "If you won't help my son, who clearly needs that help more than any of these kids, you can't help me," she stood up, raised her bandaged hand, and signed to the group, with Mike translating for her, "you can't help me."

She took my hand in hers and we went out of the room together.

I softly squeezed her hand and signed "Thank you" to her alone.

Two rehabs completed.

Mike Hicks, my mother, and I took the elevator to the ground floor.

My mother, still crying, got into the car and started it. When Mike called me over, I had just opened the door.

"Hey, man, you got a second?" He laughed.

"Ha ha, I have all the time in the world." I literally have nowhere to be."

"Listen, bro, I just want you to know, man—I get it." I understand what's going on with you. I'm not trying to lecture you; I simply want you to understand. I just wanted you to know I understand. For twenty-five years, I drank and smoked my life away. I couldn't stop myself. I harmed people. "I understand." He paused his smile and looked me in the eyes. He looked at me as if he understood. He looked at me as if I were his equal. I'd never heard an adult speak to me like way.

"I shouldn't be telling you this. You know what I mean? We are not supposed to offer our thoughts. I could get fired for this, but your mother isn't going to tell on me."

In the car, he signed to my mother, "You aren't gonna snitch on me, are you?"

My mother wiped away her tears and signed, "No."

"Look, man, I just want you to know you're not a horrible child. Sorry, you're not a nasty guy, shit, you're no longer a child. You're not a bad person. You're ill. I was once quite unwell. But I recovered. This year, my mother died at my house. I was there with her. You realize what I'm saying? She forgave me?"

I didn't mean to, but I did.

He produced a ten-year AA chip.

"I quit drinking a while ago and got my sh*t together." Just don't let anyone convince you that you're a bad guy, because you aren't. You've been disoriented. But if you need assistance, it is available. You can call me, we can meet, whatever you like. I'm simply telling you this because someone once told me the same thing. "You saved my life."

I was rattled, nearly matching my mother's sobs tit for tat. "Cool, man, I appreciate it, thanks." I turned to get into the car. Mike put his hand on my shoulder. Pantera Neck had grabbed me right there. I gave him permission.

"Remember, you're going to have to take a right turn someday." You're going to have to make a decision, you know? There will come a moment. You'll have to stroll alone. You'll have to turn right at some point. You'll have to stroll by yourself."

"Yeah, well, thanks."

He embraced me. What was he doing hugging me?

"You don't have to get good; you just have to get well." "See you later, bro."

I was at a loss for words. "Yeah, later."

I got into my car. We got in the car and drove away. My mother placed her hand on my leg. I lowered my gaze to her hand. My mother still adored me. As a result, you became one of us.

# CHAPTER 11

# "FREE"

Six months later, it was a Wednesday. Maybe it was a month later on a Tuesday. It had been a day. In the late afternoon. The fog was drifting around on the ground like an old gray rug, unrolling itself onto Oakland. The fog was everywhere, including inside of me. I'd just been kicked out of the Kaiser Adolescent Chemical Dependency Program's new Oakland location. I'd joined shortly after Walnut Creek Kaiser fired me. They expelled me and reassigned me to a very identical program closer to home. You know how you feel when you're out of town or in a foreign country and go to a chain restaurant that you might detest back home, but the familiarity provides you comfort in that moment?

This was the polar opposite of that.

I was well-versed in every trick. I'd heard everything. The walls were all covered in the same "Don't leave before the Miracle happens" crocheted wall art. I'd managed to stay sober for a few weeks, but I couldn't keep my mouth shut. I was thrown out yet again.

Another rehabilitation facility. I was a founding member. First to enroll, first to be expelled.

Three rehabs completed.

This was my existence. There had been no change. Nothing ever altered.

I used to chuckle about it. I, too, cried about it.

The lads and I were back at Rockridge BART, trying to come up with a plan. In Oakland for one more afternoon.

Donny was present. He'd been booted out of Kaiser right after me for spitting on Pantera Neck in vengeance for my expulsion.

That's my kid!

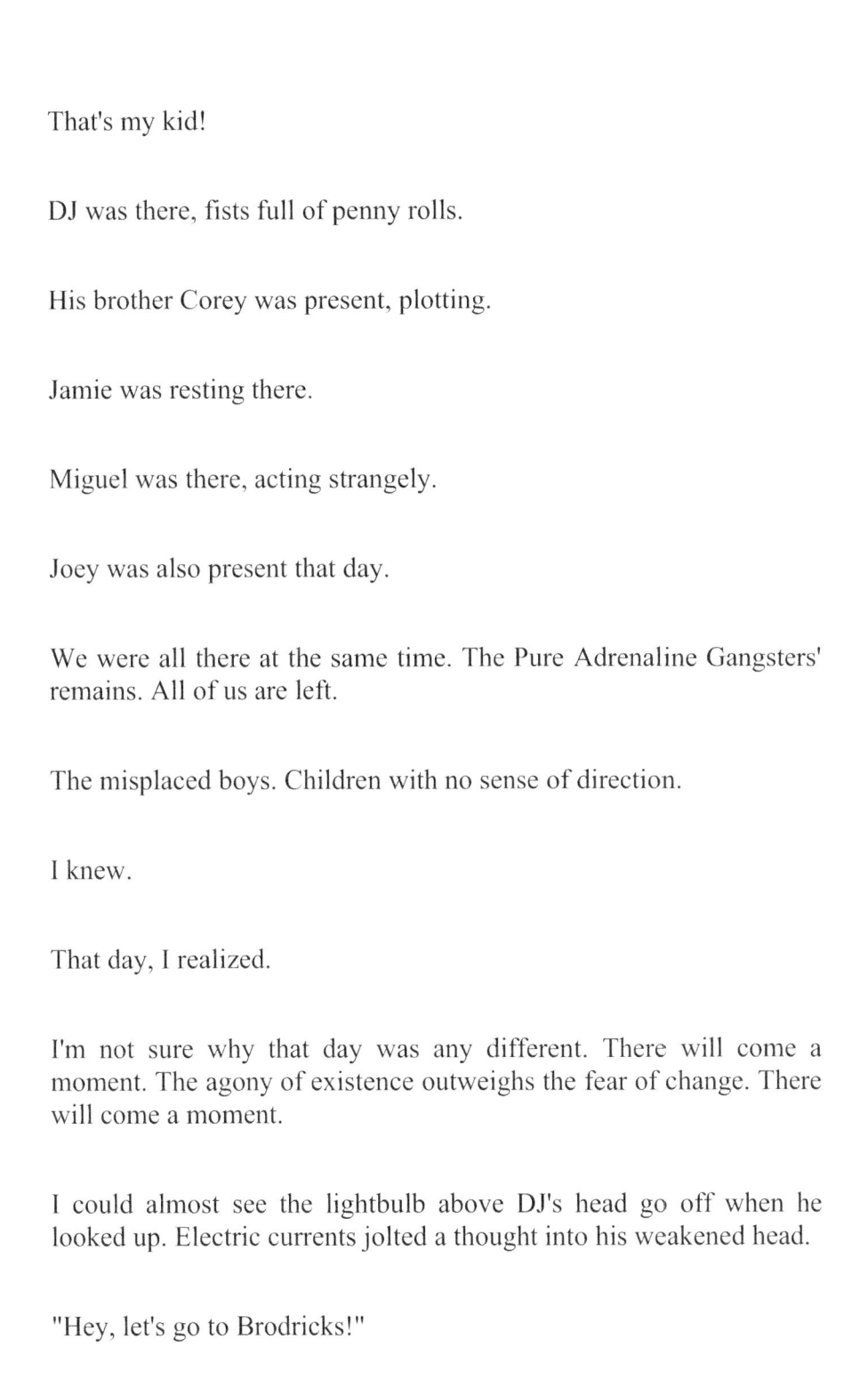

DJ was there, fists full of penny rolls.

His brother Corey was present, plotting.

Jamie was resting there.

Miguel was there, acting strangely.

Joey was also present that day.

We were all there at the same time. The Pure Adrenaline Gangsters' remains. All of us are left.

The misplaced boys. Children with no sense of direction.

I knew.

That day, I realized.

I'm not sure why that day was any different. There will come a moment. The agony of existence outweighs the fear of change. There will come a moment.

I could almost see the lightbulb above DJ's head go off when he looked up. Electric currents jolted a thought into his weakened head.

"Hey, let's go to Brodricks!"

Brodricks was a tavern we'd discovered that never appeared to card for alcohol amid the rush of after-work chaos. Regardless of how young the commuter ambling up to the pub appeared to be.

"Let's go get ripped up!" DJ was overjoyed.

Everybody was. Everyone was in agreement. Everyone. Everyone but me.

"I can't go, guys." As the words came out of my mouth, I was taken aback. I stared at the boys' perplexed expressions. These individuals. I adored these guys. My extended family.

There will come a moment.

"Huh?" DJ was perplexed. He'd had a thought. It was excellent.

"I won't be able to do it today." "I have to leave."

Donny gave me a glance. He fixed his gaze on me. Every scene from every time we'd ever shared was replaying and fast-forwarding in them. He noticed it. I noticed the difference. I noticed that something had died within me. My will had perished. My childhood had passed away. He noticed that I had finished fighting. He noticed it.

He laughed.

He grabbed my hand and slapped me with a half-hug.

"Right on, man, we'll holler atcha later." Donny locked his attention on mine. I averted my gaze.

"Of course. "Please contact me later."

There will come a moment. When you must walk alone. Take the first right.

"All right then, let's bounce." I could hear Corey drooling for a beer. I was in the same boat. My entire group of buddies turned and went away.

I took a right and walked home by myself.

I never turned around. Six months sober, at the age of sixteen, I enrolled in the Spraings Academy, another non-public school established for students who had failed in every other educational setting. I sat in the waiting area for yet another absurd dance. I'd done it a million times before. They'd talk to me, put me through tests, try to fix me, and then label me as broken. Damaged. Done.

They summoned me. I found a seat.

Dr. Violet Spraings sat across from me, and she asked me a question that no one in the educational world had ever asked.

"So, what do you want to do?" She laughed.

I considered it.

"Well, I've been a freshman for what seems like an eternity. I haven't passed a grade since seventh grade. To be honest, I'm not willing to put up with it. I'll just drop out if I have to, although I'd prefer not to. So, I think what I want is for someone to assist me in getting my GED and getting out of here."

Dr. Spraings leaned forward and locked his gaze on my. "Okay."

"Okay?"

"Okay. Let's get started. Give me the rest of the school year, and I'll set you up to be tutored all day with the goal of obtaining you your GED."

"Are you serious?"

"Totally." She smirked. "Are you?"

"What do you mean, am I?" I inquired.

"Are you going to work your tail off for me?" Will you persevere even if you want to give up again? I need you to confirm your seriousness as well."

"I'm not kidding. I swear." For the first time in my life, I realized my pledge meant anything.

"All well, then we'll do it. It will take some time for me to organize a timetable in which I can have you work one-on-one with a tutor all day. Meanwhile, you'll just have to sit in my office and read this book. But read everything well and attempt to study it. If you do, I believe you will benefit greatly from it. Deal?"

I gave a wide grin. "Deal!"

She handed me a battered crimson-covered book, and I began my first day at my previous high school. I opened the book and turned to the title page. J. D. Salinger's The Catcher in the Rye. Three years have gone. I'd returned to school and enrolled in community college when I was eighteen, only six months behind when I would've started college if I'd been a typical kid who finished from high school on time. I was ready to transfer to a university two years later. I just applied to one. The Santa Barbara campus of the University of California. I was doing well. I had a high GPA with only one weak point. I'd attempted and failed pre-algebra four times. Apparently, seventh grade is a bad time to stop studying math if you want to learn the algebra abilities that will come in helpful later in your career as a stand-up comedian. Because of those pesky math classes, I hadn't been able to complete the transfer criteria.

I applied nevertheless, thinking to myself, "Whatever, algebra, no big deal; they'll let it slide."

Apparently, the admissions office did not agree with my "let it slide" attitude. I was turned away. I filed an appeal against the verdict. I wrote to the school, outlining my background and weaknesses. I'm going to explain myself. I'll explain why. And in the final paragraph of my plea, I stated, "I'm clean and sober." I've been there for five years. Your school is teeming with alcoholics. Drunken surfers who down 40s of Mickey's malt liquor before class (remember the white boy drink?). And you require my presence at your school. Just to be me. Just to be clear. "You require my assistance."

"Okay!" they said.

Two years later, I took the stage. They called out my name and then said, "Graduating with honors."

This isn't spectacular. Many people finish college. It's fantastic for me. I looked down at my mother, who was smiling at me. I'm crying for you. I'm crying good tears right now. I told her, "I love you." She said, "I love you, too." So there are two of us. One seat was empty.

My grandmother was unable to attend due to illness. I returned to Oakland, where she was dying. I held her hand in mine and said, "I graduated college, Grandma."

She squeezed my hand and replied, "Of course you did."

Samson appears in the book of Judges. The ideal Jewish man. He smashed temple walls with his bare hands. He slaughtered an army with the jawbone of an assassin. His long flowing hair gave him incredible strength, transforming him into a Jewish Superman. And, to be honest, the Jews don't have many Supermen. My Samson was my father, despite my bitterness and anger. It's the same for everyone. But, of course, when Sampson lost his hair, he lost his power. His powerful hands had become flaccid. Each superhero has a kryptonite.My father was diagnosed with cancer in February of my twentieth year. He passed away in May. I was present. This isn't spectacular. When their parents die, a large crowd gathers. It's fantastic for me. I was never present. When I came into the hospital room, I saw my father in his complete state of helplessness. My idol had been shattered. My rage was as well. All the rage I'd ever felt seemed pointless. He was thin. So slender. My father, the dynamo, was a disaster, unable to get out of bed. His brain tumors had swelled, pressing into his ocular nerve and forcing one eye shut. A skeleton with only one eye. My face was covered in blood. My heart was struck by lightning. I couldn't take a breath. I walked out of the room, waving a pitiful hello. I had to take a breather.

"Is he afraid of me?" my father asked my brother.

I gathered my courage and returned to the room. Back to my father, whom we had abandoned in New York so many years before. "I'm here, Daddy," I told him.

"Of course you are," he replied.

"You feeling okay?" I inquired, with the answer written all over his physique.

He laughed. He raised his hands and pretended to play a sad little guitar. This is a joke for me. One more joke. I grasped his hand in mine. I gripped it tightly. I sensed him. A week has gone. My father was much more terrible. Skinnier. Closer. I'd been meaning to approach him. I wanted to apologize to him for a variety of things. Making things right. I'd prepared a formal speech, complete with recovery aphorisms and apologies. I sat down next him and informed him that I needed to speak with him. My demeanor was straightforward. My intentions were good. My approaches were abysmal. As I began into a speech about my past and the mistakes I had made, my poor, frail father did his best. But he was frail from cancer and treatment, and I was interrupted five minutes into my major apology by the sound of him snoozing. My father had dozed off. I sat calmly next to him, giggling a little at myself. I'm crying a bit to myself. I stood up to leave. My father rustled awake just then. He lifted his hands politely and signed to me. A whole sentence. He hadn't had the energy to say more than one or two words at a time in days. "Water." "Bed up." "Bed down."

He suddenly signed a stream of sentences to me that had to have sapped him. I couldn't understand what he was saying because his body was so shattered and his hands were so weak.

"I don't understand," I replied.

He kept repeating himself.

"I'm so sorry, I don't understand." I felt like a jerk. For him, this meant approaching a marathon runner at the finish line and saying, "Sorry, didn't see it, start over."

He did. I realized what you meant. "I'm so lucky that you are my son."

"I'm lucky you're my dad," I said. Tears stream down my cheeks. It was our very final discussion. It was ideal. That says it all. I was in the room when he left. The reign of the King had come to an end. He'd fallen into a coma a few days before, lifeless. I recall staring at him and praying to God to take him, thinking to myself, "He's dead already." I knew how wrong I was when his heart stopped and something else went. I sat beside my father as he breathed his last. When I looked back at him, he'd left the room. I was relieved I hadn't. In that moment, I ripped my shirt in two, as is customary in Jewish mourning. The ripping of the cloth, slicing through the room, scraping the roof of my consciousness. My father had died. The following week, I sat close to the ground, receiving visits alongside the rest of my family as we sat shiva. Shiva is a hallucinogenic experience in which you sit high on sadness while a parade of your loved one's history passes by to pay tribute. You simply sit. You sat all day hearing stories about how much people liked the person you loved. I got to hear all the stories about my father that my mother never told me. To hear what a wonderful person he could be. What a creator. What a gentleman. We sat around all day doing nothing. You are not even permitted to cook for yourself while sitting shiva. Someone prepares for you if you are hungry. They do not want you to be distracted. You simply sit. You sit in your sorrow. Local guys assemble at the house of sadness three times a day to ensure that ten men are present. A minyan, or quorum of ten men, is required to constitute a kind of express route of communication with God. A minyan is required to say Kaddish, the Aramaic prayer for the souls of the dead. You are interrupted in your sitting three times a day to stand and talk to God. To return to the Lord the stories you've heard about your loved one. To pray while standing. The time for afternoon prayer had arrived one day, and I stood, dazed, to pray once again. Mordechai Ben David, my Bar Mitzvah's Chassidic rock star, was the tenth to arrive. He removed his beautiful black coat and examined the situation. Ten was me, my brother, my father's deaf best buddy Billy, and six local penguins. At least, that's what we believed.

"We have to wait for one more man," Mordechai Ben David exclaimed.

"Why would we do something like that?" my brother wondered. "There's ten men here."

"There's nine officially," the Pig said. "The deaf one doesn't count."

This arrogant jerk refused to acknowledge another deaf man as a man in my dead father's house. I felt compelled to speak up. I needed to yell, "Get the fuck out of my father's house," but I couldn't. Grief had wrecked me, and the ghosts of my childhood terrors danced in my head. Screaming made it difficult to remain invisible. Me, the one who was usually saying something to the grownups who had harmed me, sat there helpless and ashamed. We waited for another man. We prayed to a God who had to be very disappointed. I just sat there thinking, "If I ever write a book, I'll make sure to include what an asshole Mordechai Ben David is."

We got up a week after sitting down. The soul is thought to linger in the chamber during shiva, listening all the stories about itself. My father, possibly hearing for the first time. A week later, you stand, open the door, and go around the block, releasing the souls of the deceased. Grief is particularly structured in the Jewish religion. Sitting for a week. A month without shaving, music, or parties. Every day for a year, you say the Kaddish prayer. It's actually very soothing. At a moment when you are at a loss for what to do and how to do it, there is a structure that tells you, "Don't worry, here's how."

A year has gone. It has been 365 days since my father passed. It's almost time to quit crying every day. It's almost time to utter Kaddish. I flew back to Sea Gate for the final time. Return to the past. My family had gathered there for the last time that year to say Kaddish. All we had to do was go to the synagogue led by Rabbi David Meisels, my failed savior who had directed me to Chabad years before. There was one issue. I'd grown my hair long the previous year. I had massive frizzy curls and looked like a crazy. I loved it back in Oakland. The notion of returning to synagogue like this in Sea Gate sent shivers up my spine. I had no idea what to do. I frantically ran around the house, trying to shove my hair into a ridiculously tiny fedora that had belonged to my younger half brother when he was thirteen. I looked like the Scarecrow with my hair spilling out of it, stuffing my brains back into my head. Shame was spinning about me at a thousand miles per hour. I reverted to being twelve, ashamed of who I was and how I looked. I was painfully aware that I wasn't, and that I never would be.

I then took a deep breath.

I realized I wasn't twelve years old.

I realized I wasn't being ruled by the monsters of my past.

I realized I was an adult.

It didn't matter if they were aware of my differences.

I was, after all, unique.

I removed my hat.

My hair cascaded over my shoulders like Samson's.

I regained my strength.

With my bare hands, I tore down the walls of my past.

I took a walk to shul.

I grew into a man.

I held my breath every time Donny's mother's number appeared on my caller ID, expecting her to say, "Donny's dead."

She almost did it one night.

The telephone rang.

"Hello?" Donny slept off behind the wheel. I collided with a guardrail. He was on the verge of losing his leg. "I nearly died."

He'd been awake for days, smuggling speed into Juárez, Mexico, when he awoke in the hospital.

He'd be OK.

Donny called me from New Mexico a year later to collect. I knew the area code and braced myself for the worst.

But he wasn't gone. He desired to live.

"I'm broken, bro," he said quietly.

"I understand, guy. "Please return home."

I met him at the airport. He had been sucked up and stank. For weeks, he'd been living out of a duffel bag. Capone, an emaciated and slightly vicious pit bull, was his only buddy. Donny made a right that day. I received another call from him last year.

"Come to the hospital."

I dashed over there. I took his newborn child from his arms. His wife was dozing off in the hospital bed. His mother sat across from her. I held his newborn daughter.

"She's stunning. But are you certain you don't want to use the name Moshe?"

Joey. Joey is a big guy. Joey is a big tough guy. My inspiration. The man who knocked Sean The Bomb out. The stud to end all studs. Zalante, Joey. What a gentleman. He crashed his motorcycle one day when high on coke and riding like a lunatic. Ass grinding against the gravel and crumbling beneath him. His tailbone was twisted and protruded indefinitely. It was a never-ending pain. He had been in the hospital for several months. He was in the hospital exactly across the street from the therapist I saw, the final round of therapy paid for by Oakland Public Schools funds, which lasted just long enough to demonstrate I was serious about getting better. Every week after treatment, I went to see Joey and told him about my new life, believing that my proximity to him was a supernatural sign, God's finger bringing us together. I planned to save him. I had no idea he wouldn't let me. Or that it wasn't my concern. I bore him to tears with syrupy tales of my new life, just like a newly saved Christian. He laughed. He appreciated my presence. My former hero. Joey was released from the hospital six months later. He limped along while sitting on a donut. He drank away the agony. He inhaled tablets. He was in a lot of pain. Years later, his doctor informed him that if he continued to drink, he would die. Joey left the doctor's office and locked himself in his flat. His body was discovered frozen in an easy chair in the living room. The agony is gone for good. Joey is a big tough guy.

I was bored in a meeting. I'd been attending these events for years. You've heard it all at some point. No worries, I went largely there to see friends and perhaps remind myself of where I came from. A voice from the back of the room piped out. The man they'd just summoned.

"I'm scared. For years, I've been suffering from major depression. I'm terrified and broken. I know I shouldn't be this messed up; I've been sober for almost a decade. I really need some group love right now."

I recognize that voice. I remember hearing about it somewhere. I turned around and returned to the voice. When I recognized him, he transformed from a resentful memory into a human being. I approached him after the meeting.

"Tim? "Hammock, Tim?"

"Yeah, that's me, do I know you?"

"You don't know who I am?" That's probably a good thing. You were my counselor at Kaiser and, in fact, New Bridge at one point. It was great to hear you. I completely understood. I'm sorry you're going through this. Oh, and I'm sorry for being such a jerk back then!"

Tim laughed. "You were a real jerk. It's great to see you."

He gave me a wink. He then hugged me.

I'd been a freelance sign language interpreter for years at the age of twenty-five. I worked as a stand-up comedian on the side, but it wasn't paying the bills at the time. Imagine my deaf mother and my large mouth, both of which seemed to stack the deck against me, now earning me compensated. Oakland Public Schools, the joke is on you.

One day, I received a call from the organization that dispatched me to tasks.

"At Kaiser Walnut Creek, we have a six o'clock assignment for you in the Adolescent Chemical Dependency Program." I'll send you directions via email."

"That's okay," I replied. "I know my way there."

"All well, then. "This is an appointment for a family session."

My heart was pounding as I sat in my old rehab chair, interpreting for a deaf family and their fourteen-year-old kid. A young person succumbing to addiction. Perhaps some attitude as well.

I sat passively, a conduit for their communication, a fly on the wall, as the parents spoke.

Everyone assumed I was simply another grownup, seated exactly where I was supposed to be. In my imagination, I had shrunk back to a fifteen-year-old boy who was lost, broken, and desperate. Nobody had any idea who I was. Nobody had any idea.

As I listened to the parents gripe and make excuses, I suddenly thought, "Whoa, these guys are just as messed up as their kids."

I paid attention. I agreed to sign. I recovered a little more.

The meeting came to an end.

I looked around and realized I could travel wherever I wanted. I was liberated.

The elevator made a noise.

The doors swung open.

Just as they were about to close, a hand darted in and triggered the sensor, causing the doors to reopen.

That kid got in the elevator with me.

I shifted my gaze to his.

"Can I help you, bro?" He glared at me as if I were an enemy.

He believes I am an adult. "No, I'm an adult!" It's just... I just want you to know you're not terrible; you're sick. But you can improve. I used to do it myself."

"This is a truly inspiring story, mister." Should I inform my father that the interpreter was offering me tips on how to improve? Isn't it going to get you fired?"

I burst out laughing. "Most likely. But you're not going to tell on me, are you?"

"Not if you leave me the fuck alone, starting… now."

"I got you. No worries, man. Sorry for bothering you."

I laughed to myself.

The door swung open.

The child emerged.

I saw myself in that child as he walked away angrily, an attitude in his step. I saw myself back then, irritated, young, and broken. When the elevator doors closed, I gazed at my reflection in the mirrored doors.

It was the same kid.

No. I shook my head. I took another look. I noticed the real me staring back at me. That huge wound had healed. It had recovered. The agony was gone. I was complete. I wasn't as shattered and horrible as the previous time I stood here staring at myself, wondering what had become of me. But then again, maybe I wasn't so broken. Perhaps I wasn't such a nasty kid after all. If I was, how did I become the person I was now staring at? A good person.

That's what I'd become: a good guy.

The contents of this book may not be copied, reproduced or transmitted without the express written permission of the author or publisher. Under no circumstances will the publisher or author be responsible or liable for any damages, compensation or monetary loss arising from the information contained in this book, whether directly or indirectly. .

Disclaimer Notice:

Although the author and publisher have made every effort to ensure the accuracy and completeness of the content, they do not, however, make any representations or warranties as to the accuracy, completeness, or reliability of the content. , suitability or availability of the information, products, services or related graphics contained in the book for any purpose. Readers are solely responsible for their use of the information contained in this book

Every effort has been made to make this book possible. If any omission or error has occurred unintentionally, the author and publisher will be happy to acknowledge it in upcoming versions.

Copyright © 2023

All rights reserved.

Printed in Great Britain
by Amazon